# THORNTON RAILWAY DAYS

LILLIAN KING

WITH

THE THORNTON RAILWAYMEN'S GROUP

WINDFALL BOOKS

ISBN No: 0 9530758 9 3

## Acknowledgements.

I would like to express my gratitude to all the people, too many to name individually, who contributed in any way to this book.

Special thanks go to:

The Thornton Railwaymen's Group of course, without whom it could not have been written; and especially to Sir George Sharp and Hugh Docherty who corrected my mistakes and kept me on the right lines.
Valda Hood Chin, whose idea it was, and her staff at Scotspeak.
Peter Westwater who supplied information and many of the photos;
Staff of Local History Departments, Dunfermline and Kirkcaldy Libraries;
        The Map Room, The Scottish National Library, Causewayside, Edinburgh
        Register House, Edinburgh
        The National Archives of Scotland, Edinburgh
Margaret Colville for information on Thornton Parish Church ;
Helen Welsh for proof reading.

## Introduction

When I was asked to write this book, I didn't have to think twice before accepting. My first experience of Thornton was, as a child, changing trains there on the way to Wemyss Castle Station for summer holidays. Railways were for many years a part of my life - five members of my family were railmen -and at the Railwaymen's Hut in Thornton, I was welcomed back into the tight knit railway community. The book includes only a small selection of the vast store of shared memories and experiences of the men who were part of Thornton's railway days.  This is their book. Writing it was a labour of love. I only hope I have done them justice

*Lillian King August 2000*

Printed by GHR Print & Design. Thornton
Typesetting, layout and design by Windfall Books
Published by Windfall Books

# THORNTON RAILWAYMEN'S GROUP 1995

Left to right: Hugh Docherty, Archie Scott, Andrew Henderson, Sir George Sharp, Willie Munro, Dave Mackie, Bob Masterton, Davie Skene, Alex. Abercrombie, Reuben McLean, Tammy Doherty, Peter Hutton, Andrew Caldwell, John Philp, John Matheson.

This book is dedicated to our friend and colleague Sir George Sharp

# CONTENTS

# FOREWORD

## DR. JOHN CAMERON C.B.E.

*Scotrail Chairman John Cameron (driver) with Jimmy Adams, last traction inspector at Thornton, early 1980s*

Railways have always played an important part of my life. Indeed I am sure that if I had not been a farmer and a part time railwayman I would almost certainly have been a career railwayman and a part time farmer. That is why I am most honoured and delighted to have been asked to write a foreword to this most distinguished book. All the more so when it is a book about the railways and railwaymen of Thornton who had such an important and fascinating influence on my early years of railway interest.

It was from the men at one of Thornton's sub depots - Anstruther - in the final years of steam that I learned the skills of firing and driving steam locos on the 'Coast Road'. There were three sets of men at Anstruther, all of them characters but the one man who was God to me was Tom Barbour of Pittenweem. Known as 'Big Tam', he had served abroad in the Navy for nine years and was extremely street wise and knowledgeable. He handled engines with great finesse and I tried endlessly to achieve his skills. Eventually when Anstruther closed Tam transferred to Thornton. I also was able to learn the techniques of Diesels in which Tam was equally efficient. Sadly Tam died well before retirement but I still cherish to this day many happy and exciting memories.

My next involvement with Thornton shed was when I purchased my 'own' locomotive the A4 Pacific No. 60009, which I was allowed to keep at Thornton for some time whilst it was handling various 'last' steam specials. Everyone was supportive and enthusiastic to have a Pacific 'on shed' from the shed master Dandy Mackay downwards but it was the redoubtable Willy or 'Darkie' Young who was one of the three gaffers who really took No. 9 under his wing. The number of test runs that Darkie found necessary was staggering. On one occasion, we went so far we needed two conductors to supplement the Thornton crew's already wide route knowledge!

But life is indeed full of surprises. After serving as President of the Scottish Farmers Union for some five years I was asked if I would accept a dual appointment as Chairman of Scotrail and also to represent Scotrail on the British Railways Board in London - a post which I enthusiastically accepted. Many times during my appointment did I ask and receive good sound counsel from my friend from Thornton, ex-driver George Sharp -latterly Sir George - who sadly passed away only a short time ago. By that time my own loco No. 9 was kept at the new Thornton shed and was being used so frequently that we had to undertake a programme of re-training steam drivers. At last I was in a position to ensure that Thornton men were to the fore. Out of six men to be retrained three from Thornton, Tam Galloway, Peter Hutton and Alex Abercrombie, were all passed out again on steam by traction inspector Jock Bruce from Inverness. What fun we had - as if any of these great men needed any retraining of any kind. But under the watchful eye of Thornton's traction inspector, Jimmy Adams - one of the most knowledgeable railwaymen I have met - we certainly saw a lot of country.

And that is what makes this book so fascinating and so valuable. Lillian King wisely decided that whilst she would draw the various strands together in a professional way, the railwaymen of Thornton must tell their own stories. Railways and railwaymen have a major influence on industrial and rural development in Fife - as indeed they have had in so many other parts of the country. Thankfully this book places on record the role which the railways made to our present way of life in Fife and most importantly it records for posterity the invaluable contributions from the railway men and women who made the railways work and who created the railway world which meant so much to so many of us. Civilisation is forever in their debt and this book rightly reminds us of that.

*John Cameron August 2000*

*The Union of South Africa at Markinch. The shunting engine next to it would pull it out of the shed*

# THORNTON

Thornton is a common name. In Britain there are at least ten villages with that title and another seventeen with it as part of their name. Thornton as a village in Markinch parish appears on the map first in 1827, and one legend has it that the name came from a thorn tree that grew by the Beech Inn. In fact its first recorded existence is in 1806. Alexander, eldest son of The Earl of Leven and Melville, inherited the title of Lord Balgonie on the death of his grandfather, and his father's title in 1802. In 1784 he had married Jane, the daughter of John Thornton, a wealthy London merchant. Both families were delighted, probably because of the money on one side and the title on the other, and in a letter to the family, one correspondent described Jane as 'a hawk out of a good nest.'

The two families maintained a very close relationship. Later, Jane's son, John Thornton Leslie Melville, married his cousin Harriet Thornton and after her death married another cousin Sophia. On a visit to Balgonie in January 1789, the Thorntons were accompanied by a Mr Bull, a friend of both Walter Scott and the poet Cowper. We know that Scott visited Fife regularly, as a guest at Blairadam and at Lochore. Cowper was well enough acquainted with the family to write a poem on the death of Jane's father. In a letter, Bull describes what the country side was like in winter.

'I came from Melville this morning with Mr Thornton and Lady Balgonie. The roads were very bad - full of ice and snow; and the country has a very dreary look - mountains covered with snow and valleys streaming with floods; barren heaths and moors for miles together. But all this is compensated for by the kindness and generosity of our hosts who treat us like what they are - right, generous, old fashioned nobility. The good Earl and his Countess are excellent people.'

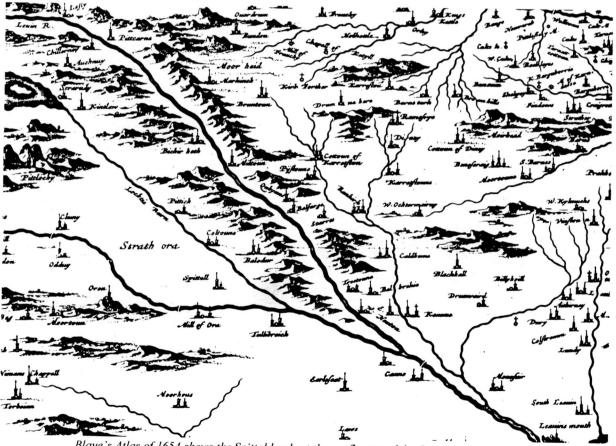

*Blaue's Atlas of 1654 shows the Spittal lands at the confluence of the Orr and Lochty Waters*
*Strathore belonged to the Countess of Rothes*

1

Bull, who was apparently a clergyman, also gives some details of the odd diet which the people enjoyed.
'We return there on Saturday and I am to preach on the Sabbath. There is great hospitality and abundance of everything that is good, but the common people get neither meat, nor butter nor honey but boiled meal with some small beer poured over it . This dish is always seen on the table. I tasted it and found it very much like the bran and water that is stirred together to feed chickens and to fatten hogs, but the great folks seem to like it exceedingly well.'

The marriage settlements of the nobility were as complicated as international treaties and six trustees, three from the Leslie family and three of Jane's brothers were appointed to oversee the contract. It was these trustees who in 1806 on Jane's behalf bought from her husband 'parts of the Lordship and Barony of Balgonie, viz. Byreton or Byresloan, Lochtyside and Spittal, Markinch now called Thornton.' The price was ten thousand pounds, payable in two instalments.

The countryside then was mostly agricultural but Thornton grew up around coal and the history of mining in this area goes back for centuries. The Coaltown of Balgonie is mentioned in a valuation roll of 1517 and the First Statistical Account for Scotland of 1795 says that 'the Earl of Leven discovered and wrought coal more than three hundred years ago.'

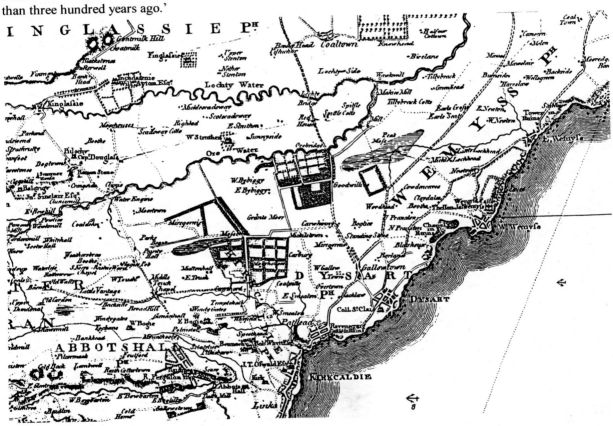

*By 1775 there is a fairly big settlement at Orr Bridge*

These were not deep pits and when the surface levels were worked out, the workings were abandoned. In 1731, Alexander the Earl of Leven began coal working again, erecting a water engine to enable coal to be dug to a depth of thirty fathoms. Later a windmill replaced the engine which could not cope with the volume of water. The Earl leased his coal works to 'tacksmen' but George Balfour of Balbirnie began digging coal on his estate in 1740 and sold it cheaper than Leslie's men could so they were forced to give up in 1743. It was over forty years before the Earl's next venture. In 1785, Lady Leven wrote to her son, Lord Balgonie, asking him to 'write to your father whenever you think anything can be done about the coal; he will turn very keen if once

*Thornton makes its first appearance on this map of 1827*

*Waukmill on the Ore*

set going; perhaps hands should be secured as they are often ill to be got, and also instruments for their work.'
The Earl was persuaded and in November 1785, a contract was drawn up with Henry Renwick to sink a coal pit at Balgonie. At that time, it was a farming and weaving community with a few small coal pits. In 1795 Markinch parish as a whole had one hundred miners and one hundred and twenty weavers. Coal had been worked in the area on a small scale since the thirteenth century but in the nineteenth century coal from newly developed pits provided steam to replace water power for the industries along the rivers Ore and Leven. Flour and meal were milled at the Ore Mill, flax manufactured at the Ore Bridge Works and Redford Factory and linseed oil produced from seed which was not good enough for planting. Other mills included Mackie's Mill and Waukmill, and a dam and sluices controlled the water supply through a mill lade to these mills.

With the coming of the railway the Fife village was named Thornton Junction to distinguish it from all the other Thorntons. Bound on one side by the River Ore and on the other by the Lochty Burn, and originally part of three separate parishes, Markinch, Kirkcaldy and Kinglassie, it became in 1877 a 'quoad sacra parish', that is a parish created for ecclesiastical purposes only. This usually happened when a parish became too large for a single minister and the original parish remained the unit for civil administration until that role was taken over by local authorities. The Reverend Mr Sievewright, minister of Markinch whose 1840 report appears in the New Statistical Account of 1845 refers to the 'new and thriving village of Thornton,' so it appears that until the industrial development of the early 19th century, the village was very insignificant. The report goes on to say that 'Originally the village owed much of its growth to a number of small coal pits which seem to have been worked at the south end of the village - Ore Bridge as it was then called. There was also a bleach field at Lochtyside, lint works and vitriol works.' These works were owned by Charles Tennant whose father was said to be a friend of Robert Burns. He began work in the weaving industry and invented a highly successful process, using chloride of lime, for bleaching linen. His main factory was at St Rollox in Glasgow and the Thornton factory was set up to save the cost of transport from there.

The 1845 account for Markinch parish gives some details of the bleach field and vitriol works. The bleach field belonged to David Landale of Kirkcaldy, and dealt with two and a half tons of linen yarn per day. It was mostly sent for manufacture in this country, but some was exported to Ireland and France. Eighty to one hundred people were employed , mostly women and girls. The women were paid 5/6 per week, men ten to twelve shillings. The bleach field stopped work in 1883 and the buildings were utilised by Hutchison Flour Millers as malting barns, but the numbers employed were few, compared with those who had worked at bleaching. The buildings were so badly damaged by subsidence that in 1950 they had to be demolished.

The 1845 report makes no mention of pits except the Balgonie which by this time belonged to

*Thornton Village 1854*

the Balgonie Coal company run by the Balfour family. In 1913 it employed three hundred and fifty workers and the company had either bought or built a considerable number of dwelling houses for their employees at Thornton, Coaltown and Milton. The Third Statistical Account, published in 1952 claimed that the last pit to be worked in the village stopped in 1847 and the map of 1854 shows Middlefield as a ruin. The Lochtyside pit

Station Road, W., Thornton

was sunk in 1846, the nearby Julian Pit began in 1883 and came into production in 1891. Steadily it expanded to reach the high-water mark in 1939 of six hundred employees and an outlet of more than a quarter of a million tons. 'Since then,' says the Account, 'both employment and production have fallen and there are now some four hundred and fifty workers. There is also a brick works at this colliery and nearly a hundred million bricks have been made.'

With the steady development of the railway system, Thornton's position as a cross-roads of natural communications took on a new importance. By the end of the 19th century, Charles Carlow, the manager of The Fife Coal company tried unsuccessfully to establish the company's headquarters there because he considered it the most convenient point between the collieries near the coast at Leven and the coal fields in Central Fife.

Four separate lines converged on Thornton Station, so that the comparatively small village quickly found itself on the map as an important railway junction. It became, and remained, largely a railway town. An account written in 1907 claimed that four hundred and forty men were employed on the railway. Though work was readily available locally for men there was little provision for women. A few were employed by the railway as cleaners and clerkesses, others found work in local shops, but the majority travelled by bus to shops, factories and offices in Kirkcaldy and Markinch.

In Mr Sievewright's day, water and sanitation were unlooked for luxuries. Water came from well-houses and in 1835, meetings were held to arrange for the North Subscription Well House to be cleaned and painted. The following year it was decided to install a pump instead of repairing the old apparatus and like careful managers, the village elders sold off the bucket and chain for five shillings, the windlass and frame for five shillings and three pence and the well creepers for eight pence. Each feuar had to pay three shillings and three pence for his share in the well and stringent rules drawn up for its use. No water was to be taken to bleach or synd clothes or any other purpose except house use, no tubs were to be allowed within ten feet of the well and people could be fined for leaving the door open. No children were to be allowed to draw water unless they were big enough to operate it properly. Later, stand pipes in the street did away with the carrying of water but it was almost into the twentieth century before drainage and sanitation schemes were put into operation. The first sewage works, built in 1898, were destroyed by subsidence in the 1930s. Subsidence was a problem which hampered the development of the village. Of the three hundred and twenty one local authority houses  built mainly for railway workers, two rows of houses - twenty two in all, and standing between the cattle marts and the station - had to be demolished in 1930 because of  subsidence. The population, which  in 1861 was five hundred and twenty seven, more than doubled to over twelve hundred in the next twenty years. In 1947,  it was a little under two thousand seven hundred, with more males than females.

Tenement buildings housed the early railway workers and overcrowding was endemic. Fast population growth led to a housing scarcity which became acute after the 1914-18 War.  Railway developments brought more people to the village, but the Railway company lagged behind the Coal Company in providing homes for the workers. Special homes were built for the station  master, the foreman and the gas inspector, Bob Thomson, known as Gassy Bob.  The housing situation was made worse by the 1939-45 War, and the fear of subsidence prevented much  development but in 1946  sixty five prefabs were built. It was anticipated that the opening of the Rothes Colliery would give rise to demands for further housing . Over the years new housing  was developed , and the village now contains a mix of private and publicly owned houses.

Subsidence also caused considerable problems for the railway company. Thornton Junction stood above a valuable coal seam and the coal company wanted £96,000 to leave the coal undisturbed but  the railway wouldn't pay. As a result, as more coal was extracted, the problems grew. Mining was taking place only one hundred and fifty metres beneath the surface and there are stories – mostly apocryphal - of miners  setting their watches by the five a.m. express going through the station, and of hearing conversations of golfers, who in turn, were said to hear shots fired and voices from underground. Mine workings caused the station - which was described in an early report as being 'notorious for its bleak and dismal aspect, especially during winter and spring months' - to subside and platforms had to be built up about five metres to compensate. Fears of subsidence meant that  until the pits closed, the line needed constant attention, trains went through the station at walking pace and a squad of men were continually ballasting the rails, which had sunk overnight, to the correct levels. The original stone buildings had to be demolished and  new light-weight wooden buildings erected in their place. The only building now to connect Thornton with its industrial past is the pit head of the old Middlefield mine which is close to the Mitchell's Homes complex. It was already a ruin when the 1854 map was printed but it still survives today, thanks to its Listed Building status.

*Thornton Station with Middlefield and the old Weighs Yard in the background*

# THE RAILWAY TOWN

Thornton was built on coal and steam and achieved its importance in railway history because of the vast deposits in the Fife coalfields. For centuries the landowners of Fife had drawn revenues and maximised the profits from the black gold under their huge estates, so it is hardly surprising that the advent of the railways, promising bigger gains through cheaper transport costs, was warmly welcomed. As early as 1836, the minister of Lindores parish could write about the benefits to the local economy of a railway system. He complained that 'Whether coals are bought at Newburgh shore or sent for to Balbirnie or other coal pits, they cost ten shillings for a single cart load.'

The middle years of the nineteenth century were a time of growth and change for the kingdom. Population almost doubled, especially in the west. New mills attracted labour from outside Fife and the rapidly growing towns provided a growing market for farm produce, which had to be carted by road or shipped from the little ports and harbours in the east. From 1842, when women and children were banned from working underground, improvements in miners' working conditions brought increased production, coupled with an awareness of the potential reserves in what was to be one of Scotland's largest coal fields. Its limited exploitation could not, however, be expanded much without an alternative and superior form of transport. The Auchterderran area, for example, had an average annual output of over 120,000 tons, about ninety per cent of which had to be carted over very inferior roads to the nearest ports. It was calculated that with rail freight the cost of shipment to Perth could be reduced by seven shillings per ton and to Edinburgh, by possibly three shillings. If the railway plan went ahead, it was also reckoned that production could increase ten fold.

*A North British Railway engine at the turn of the century*

Railways, or more accurately, wooden wagon ways with horses to draw the wagons had been used in Fife for many years within the mining industry, notably by the Earl of Elgin who owned harbours at Charlestown and Limekilns. His railway was built in 1812 and in 1834, he provided the first train to carry goods and passengers in Fife on a branch line built between Dunfermline and Charlestown. Further round the coast, until Sir Robert Henderson built a harbour at St David's in 1752, coal had been carried along the old coal road from Fordell Castle to Hillend and from there to the port at Inverkeithing. Gradually Fordell's wooden rails were replaced by iron ones and in 1853, an extension was built to join up with the recently opened Edinburgh, Perth and Dundee Railway.

The proposal for a railway system in Fife was first mooted at a meeting in Cupar on October 13th, 1840 and as well as representatives of all the major towns in Fife the provosts of Forfar and Arbroath were present. The proposal said that the formation of the railway was 'not only a measure of great national importance but is also one that cannot fail to be productive of most important benefits to agriculture and to the proprietors of minerals upon the line but also to the commercial and manufacturing interests of Fifeshire and conterminous counties.'

The initial plan was for a line from Burntisland to Cupar via Kinghorn, Kirkcaldy and Dysart and on to Dundee. It also included a line from Kettle to Perth but because another company had plans for a Stirling Perth railway, they decided not to proceed with this. The company was named The Edinburgh and Northern so the possibility of a Perth line was not entirely relinquished. The first section of the railway, thirty seven miles long, was to run from 'a point on the north shore of the Firth of Forth by way of Cupar to a point on the Firth of Tay near Ferryport on Craig.'

Plans were also drawn up for an Auchterderran branch line because a survey of the coalfields there reported 'a superior quality and extent of the Clunie, Dundonald, Lochgelly and Lumphinnans coal' and concluded that the branch railway to these collieries would be of the greatest advantage to the country and a source of considerable income. The 'all but inexhaustible' deposits of coal would afford a supply of 250,000 tons for two hundred and fifty years and the new smelting works at Lochgelly would see an increase in the traffic in pig iron. Other links planned were branch lines to Dunfermline, to St Andrews and Newburgh and ferry services across the Tay.

The railway would eventually connect Fife with Perth, Edinburgh, Dundee and the north of Scotland. Perth, it was said, would benefit especially because it was 'bereft of coal' and their agriculture would be much improved by imports of lime from Fife.

*Markinch station before the platform was extended. C1870*

It was, from the beginning, recognised that one of the chief depots on the line would be required near Markinch for 'the accommodation of The Water of Leven traffic.'

The prospectus for The Edinburgh and Northern Railway was drawn up and carefully revised and the plans lodged, but 'a general stagnation of commercial relations' induced the committee to hesitate till the money market and trade in general began to recover before they would go ahead. Meantime, advertisements were placed in Liverpool, Manchester, Newcastle and London papers as well as Edinburgh and 'the Scotch provincial papers.' Care had to be taken that the right sort of person should be accepted as shareholders. By October 1844, sixteen thousand , five hundred shares worth £412,725 had been sold. By the time the Bill was presented to Parliament the company's ambitious plans were being upset by other proposals that had been put forward. The Edinburgh and Perth Railway planned a route to South Queensferry, then from North Queensferry to Cowdenbeath and on to Glenfarg and Perth, with branches diverging to Kirkcaldy and Dunfermline. Fortunately for the Edinburgh and Northern, the other company's plans were so badly prepared that their application was thrown out. In 1845, 'railway mania' led to sixteen railway schemes being presented, by a variety of newly formed companies, to the Sheriff Clerk of Fife but only a few were successful.

*B1 passing Glenfarg on the way to Thornton*

Before a railway could be built, an Act of Parliament was necessary and many schemes were refused because insufficient research had been done on costing, planning and projected income but, in 1845, permission to go ahead was granted to the Edinburgh and Northern Railway. As well as properly executed plans, they had the backing of some of the most powerful men in the country. The first management committee included a collection of Earls - of Leven and Melville, Falkland, and Glasgow as well as Sir John Richardson of Pitfour Castle, John Balfour of Balbirnie and a number of Edinburgh business men, including John Thomson of the Royal Bank of Scotland. His presence on the board might have accounted for the company's funds being transferred from the Union Bank to the Royal. The capital in 1844 was £600, 000 and shares were offered at twenty five pounds each. No-one was eligible to serve on the committee unless he had at least ten shares.

*Thornton Junction c1894. Engine 110 —.40 to Leven on left. Engine 598 7.35 Edinburgh-Aberdeen on right.*
*Inspector Williamson in foreground*

*Thornton Station staff c1890*

Landowners in Fife were encouraged to become shareholders and most were happy to join. They did so, however, on the understanding that they reserved the right to determine the price of their land and how the line should run through their estates. Sir John Richardson, for example, objected to a bridge which would go through his best fishing so he was allowed to change the route. Captain Wemyss who initially objected in principle to the whole scheme was co-opted on to the committee. He agreed on condition that he could make alterations to the proposed line but showed his gratitude by persuading Lord Rosslyn to take part in the venture. The Captain was given a seat on the board and later paid £15,000, probably as compensation for 'inconvenience'. Minutes of meetings are dotted with references of such payments to various landowners. Provost Swann of Kirkcaldy promised the townspeople's support and asked that the station be placed near the harbour. The first stage of the line from Burntisland to Markinch was opened in 1846 and reached Cupar the following year.

The opening ceremony took place on September 17th before an audience of about seven hundred people and with, according to The Scotsman, 'an unlimited amount of champagne.' The Cupar to Ferryport section was completed in May 1848. The branch from Thornton to Dunfermline was opened as far as Crossgates the same month, with coach connections to Dunfermline, and goods traffic began about the same time. In 1847, the Edinburgh and Northern joined the Edinburgh, Leith and Granton Railway Company to become The Edinburgh, Perth and Dundee Railway and in 1862, was amalgamated with The North British.

*Engine used for taking trucks to and from Burntisland and Granton ferry boats.*
*Similar ones were used at Tayport. Photo taken at Ladybank where it was used for shunting.*

Within a few years, because of the steady increase in mineral traffic, Thornton had become one of the most important stations on the line. Coal production increased at such a rate that the wagons available could not cope with the demand and the railway company had to invest in coal storage areas in all the larger stations throughout the mining districts. The 1862 half yearly report said that 369,000 tons of goods and coal and 835,000 passengers were carried over seventy eight miles of track. The biggest problem of sending goods to Dundee and Edinburgh by rail and ferry was that shipments had to be handled no less than six times during transit, being loaded and unloaded and this was expensive and time consuming as well as adding to the risk of damage to more fragile cargoes. This problem was solved in 1850 by Thomas Bouch, later to become infamous as the designer of the ill fated Tay Bridge.

Bouch's solution was to invent a floating railway. At each pier, rails and slip ways were laid which could be raised or lowered by winches according to the tides. Railway lines were laid on the deck of an enormous paddle steamer, the Leviathan, and the first roll on roll off ferry was born. The first steamer ferry crossing from Burntisland to Granton in February 1850 took less than an hour and four or five return trips were made daily. The Leviathon's three tracks could accommodate thirty four wagons and 75,000 were carried annually for the next ten years. In 1862, 42,460 wagons were ferried over the Forth and by 1887, that number had doubled. A second ferry service between Tayport and Broughty Ferry began in March 1851. Burntisland was a busy port. As well as the ferry trade there was a thriving coal export trade to Denmark, Germany and the Baltic ports and imports of esparto grass, flax, linseed and straw. Until 1888, Burntisland had been the only major coal port but that year, the first dock was opened at Methil by Captain Randolph Wemyss. The railway from Thornton to Buckhaven, opened in 1881, was extended to Methil and the new station opened to passengers on 5th May, 1887, the same day as the opening ceremony for the dock.

Towards the end of the century there was a terrific upsurge in coal production. New coal mines were sunk, with ever deeper shafts and an influx of miners from the west, notably from Lanarkshire, pushed up the

*The Tay Bridge and Wormit Station c 1900*

population of mining villages to new heights. The vast increase in coal traffic meant that very soon, the Methil dock could not cope and by 1900, another dock, capable of dealing with the fifteen hundred or so ships and over 1.6 million tons of coal that were exported annually, was opened. In ten years that figure doubled and a third dock was opened in 1913. In 1923, Methil provided facilities for two thousand, nine hundred and thirty four vessels and exported nearly three and a half million tons of coal. At the same time, the railway approaches to the docks had to be completely re-organised and new lines built.

New railway companies were formed to take advantage of the boom in trade. The Alloa, Dunfermline and

Kirkcaldy Railway hoped to set up new harbours and docks at Kirkcaldy, with a line running through Dunfermline, Inverkeithing, Aberdour and Auchtertool, but although agreement was given for the work to go ahead, this project foundered. Other activities flourished, though. The second Tay Bridge, replacing the disastrous first attempt, was opened in 1887 and the Forth Bridge in 1890, both providing alternatives to the ferry crossings. New lines were opened, existing ones upgraded and double tracks laid and by 1904 the railway lines were serving eighty two collieries and over ninety factories throughout Fife. Holiday traffic was in its heyday with special tourist trains being added to the normal busy schedule. During World War One, military establishments were set up in various places within easy distance of North British lines as well as garrisons to protect the Forth and Tay bridges, and thousands of men and horses were carried south by special trains. When the army was mobilised in August 1914, signal boxes which normally closed over the weekend had to stay open and special arrangements were made for three military special trains from Dunfermline to stop at Carlisle so the horses could be watered. Trains on the North British line carried two hundred and sixty thousand men bound for France and another seven hundred thousand within the UK. Special leave trains went between Rosyth, Invergordon, Thurso and other naval bases and two thousand journeys were made daily between Rosyth, Edinburgh and Dunfermline. During the construction of Rosyth Dockyard twenty four workmen's trains arrived daily from those towns and when the entire Grand Fleet was given leave at Christmas 1918, thirty two specials carried men from Rosyth and Port Edgar.

*The old loco shed (closed 1933)*

At the centre of all this activity was Thornton. As early as 1865, its importance as the hub of the soaring mineral traffic had been recognised. In 1880 it had two engines. In 1894 a new shed, subsequently to be known as the old shed, opened with sixteen engines, four new roads, a turntable and a coal stage. In 1898, two private firms built wagon repair shops on the site and in 1923, a wagon repair works was erected near the old locomotive shed for the repair of the Company's own rolling stock . Both were still in operation in 1952, employing over a hundred men. The railway company also had a small gas plant for the use of the station and shunting yards. By 1907, a total of four hundred and forty men were employed in and around Thornton Station and the best paid were the engine drivers, who earned twenty four shillings a week.

The station was enlarged, with extra platform space being provided and waiting and refreshment rooms were built. Eventually the facilities for passengers included a fruit stall, a kiosk for papers and tobacco and a platform service of fruit and books. Coal , though the most important commodity that the company's success was built on, was not the only one. It was said that everything from cows to coffins was carried by train. For a time the herring trade from Crail and Anstruther had a good run but that didn't last long. Horses were transported to race meetings throughout Fife. Loading banks had to be built to cope with the loading and unloading of approximately two hundred cattle and two hundred and seventy sheep which were sold every week.

In 1895, two firms of auctioneers, John Swann & Sons and Messrs MacDonald, Fraser & Sons had set up an auction mart and sales were held every Monday with livestock from all over Fife. This market continued , though on a much smaller scale into the 1950s. Much of the traffic was with the butchery trade in Glasgow. When it was in full production, the sugar refinery at Cupar took delivery of more than one hundred thousand tons of sugar beet, over eleven thousand wagon loads in a three month harvest period. Seed potatoes also provided income as, on a much larger scale, did whisky from Haig's plant in Markinch and the paper mills at Leslie and Auchmuty. The RAF station at Leuchars was supplied with thousands of gallons of aviation fuel from BP's Grangemouth refinery.

*North British engine driver pre 1900*

*By 1933, when work on a new engine shed was completed, Thornton had one hundred engines. The shed took three years to complete, measured 360 feet by 106 feet and could accommodate thirty six engines on six running lines. It was opened in July 1933 by Miss Whitelaw, daughter of the Chairman of the LNER and aunt of William Whitelaw, who was later a minister in the Thatcher government. In 1953, Thornton still ranked as the fifth largest engine depot in Scotland.*

# LAST DAYS

Until the second war, half of the coal produced in Fife went abroad and had been carried direct from pit to port, but with plans to double the output, it was necessary to develop a series of marshalling yards for the stockpiled fuel. A number of small yards were built but most of the coal and goods traffic continued to be handled in six small yards or groups of sidings near Thornton Station. The working of these sidings were not very efficient so in 1957 a new mechanised marshalling yard was brought into use at Redford near Thornton Junction. The new marshalling yard, the third and largest stage of marshalling yard development and modernisation in Fife in many years, measured approximately seventy eight acres and cost in the region of £1,350,000 with some fifteen miles of sidings and twenty seven miles of track in all.

*Thornton North End*

The yard, expected to be one of the most modern in Europe was on the Dunfermline Thornton route, west of Thornton Junction, and lying to the north side of the main line and with a direct connection to the new Rothes Colliery which was being developed by the National Coal Board .A new signal box was to be built to control the supply of empty wagons to the Colliery. The new yard was planned to absorb the large increase in output arising through expanding development of the Fife coal field and would also take the place of the separate groups of sidings which could not be satisfactorily extended and modernised. Eventually, the number of wagons to be dealt with in the new yard was expected to reach 3,000 daily, an increase of one hundred per cent over the current level of traffic. Incoming trains at Thornton were routed into six reception sidings and after passing over the hump, each cut of wagons ran into one of thirty five sidings, each of which held fifty five wagons . The speed of each wagon was accurately controlled by two sets of automatically operated and adjusted pneumatic rail brakes. Primary and secondary speed retarders ensured that wagons moved rapidly and safely down the gradient and over the points into their pre-selected sidings.

This form of speed control to be adopted at Thornton was the first of its kind in Great Britain, though the system had been in use in America since 1952. Radar techniques were used to measure wagon speed and feed the information back to the control tower. Special lighting was provided to enable round the clock working. In addition there were up and down direction departure lines, an up arrival line, a train engine release line and a siding for brake vans. It also provided a seventy foot electrically operated turntable, brake-van sidings and wagon repair facilities. Altogether it could accommodate three hundred wagons on its reception lines while the sidings could hold over two thousand.

*Thornton Shed east end with shed master's office in fore ground
and coaling plant in the background.*

Thornton was chosen for various reasons. It held an important position in relation to most passenger and freight lines in Fife with sixty passenger trains a day rising to eighty four in summer; it was a half way point between Edinburgh and Dundee; there was already a large railway community - three out of every four houses in the village were occupied by railwaymen and it had a power depot nearby. Most importantly, perhaps, it was close to the new collieries and open cast sites which were then under construction. Rothes Colliery, where production was expected to reach 5,000 tons per day by 1960, was directly connected to the east end of the Yard, whilst the Westfield Opencast Site, one of the largest in Britain, could be reached by a four mile long mineral line. It was expected that the demands of the two new generating stations at Kincardine and Longannet would be catered for by the expansion of the Seafield, Comrie and Valleyfield pits. Westfield open cast mine was also to provide an important source of suitable coal for Fife's two new power stations. Kincardine, opened in October 1960, consumed eight thousand tons of coal a day. Longannet needed twenty thousand tons to maintain its output. Traffic went from Thornton Yard north east by the Tay Bridge to Dundee and Aberdeen, northwards to Perth and Inverness, and west to the Glasgow area and expanding markets were forecast.

In 1953, Fife council planners were discussing the anticipated expansion of the mining industry. There were over twenty two thousand miners in Fife and it was expected that in the year 2000, there would still be three thousand miners between Bowhill and Kinglassie. A new influx of migration was taking place from Lanarkshire. Glenrothes, built to service the Rothes Pit, was planned on the basis of a balanced population - one miner to every eight houses instead of being concentrated in mining villages.

Looking back it is easy to recognise why these projections were false but at the time, with the information available, and no indication that a contraction and consolidation programme was about to be put into effect by the Coal Board, the future seemed bright. Within ten years, however, there was a rapid and catastrophic decline in the coal mining industry in Fife. The much vaunted Rothes Pit - the last development planned by the Fife Coal Company before its demise in 1947, the first sod cut by Augustus Carlow, Chairman of The Company, the day before the mines came into public ownership - had been a total disaster, one predicted by local miners who knew it had been sunk in the wrong place. The motto of the new town of Glenrothes, built to house the Rothes miners, was Ex Terra Vis -out of the earth, power. Bill Reid a Latin teacher provided a new one - Ex Terra Aqua - out of the earth, water. From the beginning it was a white elephant which produced more water than it did coal and millions of pounds of public money went down its gaping maw. The number of working collieries in Fife was reduced to only seven and all possibility of growth had disappeared. Twenty thousand jobs were lost in five years. Only four collieries, the Michael and Seafield in east Fife and Comrie and Valleyfield in the west of the county, were expected to continue operating into the 1970s. The Michael, however, was closed after a disastrous explosion in 1967 and by the following year the Thornton Yard was shut each weekend from 6.00 a.m. on Saturdays until 2.00 p.m. on Mondays.

*When coal was still king. This is now the site of the new station*

Several things brought about the decline of Thornton Junction and these are closely interlinked. First and most important was the collapse of the coal industry, which to a large extent took away its reason for being. As early as 1955, cheap coal from Poland was being unloaded at Burntisland, partly for household use and partly for use by British Rail. Cheap oil imports from the middle east and the growth of car ownership meant a decreasing passenger market, while the growth of the road haulage industry reduced the demand for freight. One stop deliveries from factory to shop were seen as more efficient. The opening of the Forth and Tay Road Bridges and the burgeoning development of bus companies meant even fewer rail passengers. At the same time, clean air legislation was coming into effect and with it the move to 'cleaner' forms of energy nuclear rather than fossil fuel driven. The discovery of gas under the North Sea spelled the end of coal gas and with it the end of the Lurgie gasification plant at Kinglassie which used a lean gas produced from open cast coal laced with butane imported by tanker from Milford Haven. Trains which had carried coal to gas plants in Perth , Inverness , Dundee and Aberdeen were no longer needed. Since Thornton basically existed on the movement of coal, the effect was catastrophic. At the same time, diesel engines were being introduced, which had a double effect. Coal was no longer required and, eventually, single manning became the norm. Though steam and diesel worked in tandem for a time, the time for steam was running out. When British Rail took over the railways in Fife in 1947 there were two hundred and thirty four miles of passenger track and seventy eight stations. Within a few years, forty eight miles of track had disappeared and by 1980 the figures had gone down to eighty one and eighteen. In 1948, Thornton had been the busiest station on the line with eighty five trains entering or leaving every day. When the station closed to passenger traffic in October 1969, only ten trains were passing through each day.

At its peak, Thornton Station was busy enough to employ two inspectors, a foreman, thirteen porters and eight ticket collectors. In 1953, the engine shed was the fifth largest in Scotland. In 1965, when nine Fife pits had been closed , there were still forty steam engines working coal trains but as closures continued, steam locomotives became redundant and most were sold for scrap. The Thornton shed shut in April 1970, its door closing on one hundred and twenty five years of steam history.

*The end of the line. Steam engines being shunted for scrap at Inverkeithing*

# THE ENGINE DRIVERS' STORY

## HUGH DOCHERTY

*It may have been every schoolboy's dream to become an engine driver but it was not an easy one to achieve. Because the railway offered a job for life, or at least till retirement age, promotion was slow and for most of the Thornton men, who joined the railway in the 1940s, their apprentice ship could last for twenty years. There had been a huge influx of men after the First World War and the average length of service was fifty years so there was little movement within the ranks for a very long time. Drivers and firemen worked unsocial hours, starting and finishing every hour of the day or night, with about fifty two different shifts and never two weeks the same, which meant that any regular family and social life was extremely difficult. Drivers travelled, by bicycle mainly, from Ladybank, Methil, Kirkcaldy and West Fife. In spite of this, for most loco men, theirs was a labour of love. Hugh Docherty spent forty eight years working on the railway but never lost the fascination for trains, and especially steam engines which began when he was a boy at Denend School.*

Like every schoolboy it was always my dream to be an engine driver. Denend school was close to Cardenden Station and every break and lunch time, we'd watch the trains. They all stopped at Cardenden and there was always lots of activity with all the coal and passenger traffic. Quite a lot were booked times for running, others were conditionals which were worked to control orders and were fitted in between passenger trains. They went up to Bowhill, the Minto and Lumphinnans to pick up coal. There used to be a train shunt at Glencraig, just along from Cardenden, which was the junction going into Bowhill, Glencraig, Brighills and Dundonald, and Bob Wilson and I used to go along after school . One of the drivers, Tom Thomson, known as Hurricane because he was always in a hurry, used to take us up on the engine and give us a run into Glencraig or Bowhill. We had to hide because if the signalman saw us, the driver would be reported. No-one except the driver and fireman were allowed on the foot plate.He'd slow down when we came out of Bowhill and let us off on the blind side of the signal box so we could get down the banking without being seen.

*Hugh Docherty with railway buddies in Germany*

When I left school, I went to Dick's Co-operative grocer's shop, then to the dockyard as an apprentice electrician before starting on the railway. I started at Lochgelly as a demurrage checker. All the coal wagons were privately owned by different coal companies but the railway had to move them when they were loaded with coal. If they stood more than twenty four hours the company had to pay a demurrage tax. I had to go around checking the wagons - their destination, the company name, date etc. Penalties were imposed if they weren't moved within a certain time. Some stood for two or three weeks so a lot of money could be made

After eight months at Lochgelly, I began as a cleaner at Thornton Motive Power Depot, and I began the long apprenticeship through the various stages of footplate promotion, finally becoming a driver twenty years later in 1964. Once in my first days as a driver, the foreman instructed my fireman and myself to prepare a specially selected locomotive to work the Royal Train on a visit to Wemyss Castle, on one of the Queen's visits to Fife. I remember feeling honoured, but apprehensive, hoping that all would go to plan.

*Hugh Docherty with William Arnott preparing to work the engine for the
Royal train from Thornton to Wemyss castle*

When they started National Service I was one of the first to go, in March 1947, during the worst winter in living memory. We did our training with The Seaforth Highlanders at Fort George and we didn't think we were going to get there. Our first job was to clear six feet of snow from the parade ground. After basic training, I was posted to Longmoor Camp in Hants, home of a military railway – just what I wanted. After two weeks, I was again on the move to Detmold in Germany, where the Army had its main railway training headquarters and had trains working over the German main line, which was just starting to recover after the War. After a few weeks in the training school, I was passed as a driver, and we worked passenger and freight trains with German drivers to teach us the route and signals. Mostly it was military routes but on certain sections we ran through civilian lines. I spent the rest of my Army time at Detmold.

After being demobbed in 1949 I returned to Thornton Depot and regained my own place on the fireman roster. After a while I went on to become a driver, and in 1982 I applied for a Train Crew Supervisors post at Thornton. After I was promoted I spent most of my time In Edinburgh Waverley Station on loan from Thornton. I found it a bit hectic after working at Thornton, but enjoyed the challenge.

## ANDREW HENDERSON

*Andrew retired in 1988 after spending forty one years on the railway. Taken on as a cleaner, he worked his way up to engine driver and supervisor. He is unusual in that he had no family connections with the railway and had another career before he went to work at Thornton.*

I left school at fourteen and worked for a time as a barman in The Auld Hoose in Kirkcaldy before going to the shipyard. I served my time as a driller at Burntisland. I had an accident and was off work for nine months and by that time I was wanting to get away so I was quite glad to get my call up papers. I joined HMS Ganges which was like a concentration camp but it didn't do me any harm. My first shore base was HMS Robertson, the 45th Marine Commando base at Sandwich in Kent, which was supposed to be a secret camp but it was always under shell fire. We had no fires in our hut and you lay in your hammock at night with the snow coming through the roof. Our Christmas dinner was cold spam. I saw a notice asking for volunteers for coastal forces so I joined and did my training at Fort William then went to Great Yarmouth, We were in Normandy for D-day and spent about fifteen days there living on corned beef sandwiches. It was a bit hair raising. We went trips to the Hook of Holland, Norway and the Adriatic Coast. When the war finished we were paraded in Great Yarmouth and given forty-eight hours leave. With a friend, I went to London to join in the celebrations and that lasted a week. When we got back to base we found everyone was on leave except for Jimmy the One and he was drunk, so I made out seven day leave passes for both of us and we went home. Next stop was Chatham. There were thirty-eight thousand men there so I couldn't believe it when I heard my name called over the tannoy. The chief drafting officer was married to a girl from Kirkcaldy and he offered me the choice of two ships - one going to Durban, the other in Rosyth. It had been in the yard two years waiting for repair. I thought that would do me, I'd be close to home, It didn't work out like that and three months later, I was in the Mediterranean and it was quite some time before I got home again.

When I left the navy, I hoped to finish my time at the ship yard but, though according to government rules they had to take me back, they made it clear that I'd be sacked as soon as my time was out. The railway job

*Royal train heading for Markinch. Photo taken from the footbridge at Thornton Station*

came about through a chance conversation at a bus stop. There was a problem at the coal yard at Thornton and wagons were having to be loaded by hand. When that job finished, I was taken on as a cleaner and worked my way up to engine driver and supervisor before I retired.

*The Royal train with Thornton North End Bothy in the background. The four headlamps denote the Royal Train*

I once drove the royal train from Perth to Aberdour. The Queen was visiting Mossmorran and I was supposed to join the train at Dalmeny but there was a bomb scare on the Forth Bridge so the train was diverted to Perth. Hugh Docherty was the supervisor at the time and he had to drive me to Perth to get the train. We came from Perth via Lindores and I had to pick a spot to stop so the Queen could have her breakfast and exercise the corgis. It was to have been near Collessie but I was instructed to stop between the two level crossing gates at Ladybank, right on the golf course. Now, it was supposed to be a secret, nobody knew the Queen was going to Perth but when we stopped, there were about a hundred people with cameras. So somebody else had to take the dogs out.

How did I get picked? Well, I had a good record. I got told a week before and I was given a whole case of stuff that I had to read and keep private. I also had to sign the Official Secrets Act and couldn't even talk to the wife about it. It was an enjoyable experience. It was a diesel class 47 with about ten coaches, and though I didn't see inside it, I was told that there was a wireless room where they could keep in touch with anywhere in the world. The Queen's coach was right next to the engine and I had to stop on the exact spot on Aberdour platform so she could step out on to the red carpet. There was no room for manoeuvre.

My wife was more worried about it than I was because we'd seen an occasion on television when the driver had missed the red carpet and all the people had to run to rearrange things. She was a secretary in the management Department of the College and couldn't settle to do any work. Colleagues were trying to pump her for information and her stock went up enormously. I wasn't nervous. I was driving a train with an important person in it, but just doing my job. I maybe took a little more care than usual about speed limits. Between Burntisland and Aberdour there's a place that's bad for leaves. If you're going slow and hit wet leaves, you lose your feet, the wheels just birl. If you're that wee bittie faster the momentum will keep you going so I increased speed a bit and it worked out fine. We arrived dead on time.

# DAVID MACKIE

*The railways are in David Mackie's blood, and he has a long and proud connection with the industry. Three generations of his family have been engine drivers . One of his last jobs was to drive the final direct train between Fife and Glasgow. 'We went over the Forth Bridge, then on to the loop through Winchburgh in West Lothian. Nowadays, if you want to go to Glasgow from Fife, you have to go to Edinburgh first.'*

My grandfather joined the railway in 1874 and retired in 1928 at seventy years old. He was one of the first drivers of the Fife Coast Express that ran from Crail to Glasgow.  Anstruther was a sub-depot to Thornton, and that's where his engine was kept. He was on duty early morning with his fireman to prepare his engine which took three quarters of an hour. Then light engine to Crail for carriages, then proceeded to Glasgow. He was well known to all his workmates for his cheeky but cheery nature and was nicknamed, 'Auld Tammy'. In his later years, he became the driver of the carriage Pilot at Thornton. He was a great Union man, and I think he was the third member of  ASLEF (Associated Society of Locomotive Engineers and Firemen).

*William Mackie, driver. S. Bloomfield, Guard c1915*

Both his sons became drivers. Andrew died in his early years, but did twenty six years of service. George, started at Thornton Loco-Depot, but emigrated to Canada, became a driver there and then retired after serving forty eight years.  The younger daughter , my mother, married William Mackie, my father. He worked on the railway at Thornton for forty six years, was also a great Union man and  one of the men who started Mutual Improvement Classes at Thornton. When I was seventeen years old, my father took me down to the loco sheds to see about a job as a cleaner, I was accepted and started work on 6th May, 1935. 1 worked all summer and was paid off at the end of the year. I remember the day I started. When I was leaving the house, my Grandfather, Old Tammy, gave me money in an envelope. I think it was a shilling or two, and he told me to go to D. Laing, Secretary of ASLEF and tell him that a good condition of service was better than a shilling a day.
In April, 1936, I started work again, not at Thornton, but at Perth Loco Depot. My wages at that time were one pound three shillings and my digs were one pound, but we got a weekend travel pass to get home. I was lucky that my parents were in a position to give me pocket money, and Mother always had three twenties ciga-

rettes in with my clean washing. I first started work as a fireman at Perth Loco Depot. I was there for two years, then I was sent back to my home depot at Thornton and it was not long before I was made permanent fireman. In 1940, Dunfermline Loco Depot was really very busy; they were getting all the extra work and were putting up vacancies every week for firemen. I think about fifteen Thornton men transferred to Dunfermline, and again I landed in digs with a Mrs McIver, who had a family of her own, but I was treated as one of them. My parents became their life-long friends. Mr McIver was a Master Coach Painter and Sign Writer, and later worked at Rosyth Dockyard.

We were supposed to do air raid duties once a week, but I did not need to do mine very often as I was working overtime nearly every shift and doing three Sundays out of four. I worked approximately eighty hours in a seven day week , finishing at 4.30 pm on the Saturday afternoon. We used to work what they called Liberty Trains from Rosyth Dockyard to Edinburgh Waverley. There were four or five of those trains daily, with thirteen coaches on, with workers and sailors from the shore base. We used to work the workers' trains in the mornings and at tea time, along with trains from Thornton Depot. They started from Markinch, Leven, Dysart, Kirkcaldy, Cardenden, and they all had nine and ten carriages, and all went into Rosyth Dockyard, except two which were Donibristle specials. In those days, we had something like thirty-five to forty engines at Dunfermline Depot, and ninety-eight engines at Thornton Depot. I got a transfer back to my home Depot at Thornton, and worked with my father as his Fireman on passenger trains such as the Fife Coast Express, which ran from Leven to Glasgow, and also Dundee and Edinburgh. That's where I learned most of my knowledge of driving duties such as engine failures, and how to deal with them.

A year or two later, I got a letter to go to Burntisland to sit my driving test, which was an ordeal, to go in front of John Allen, Chief Loco Inspector who in later years became the Lord Provost of Dunfermline. It was not very long before I was appointed Permanent Driver, but it would take a book to tell you all about the ups and downs of being a driver. But I often think about all the great lads that fired to me on the engines. I took early retirement in August, 1979. I am still very much in touch with the railways, although it has been very sad throughout the years since the Beeching Plan was introduced. I particularly remember one week of work in 1978, I was the driver on the afternoon Thornton to Glasgow Queen Street train which was a diesel triple set. This was to be the last week for direct travel from Fife to Glasgow. On the Saturday, I went on duty and took my camera with me, but I really thought there would be someone of authority at the Station, to see the last train off, but there was nobody, and when I arrived at Queen Street Station, the same blank platform confronted me. I stood there for a wee while and wondered, does nobody care any more for trains or people?

The guard then came forward with his kit, and he said to me, "Is there no-one here either?" With that I saw a platform inspector, I went over to him and told him the story. He admitted that he had never heard of this, I asked him if he would take a photograph of the guard and me. He took the photograph, handed the camera back and walked off. I thought, what a way for nearly a century of dedicated service to be brushed off.

*Driver David Mackie with Fireman W. Peebles and Guard G. Mitchell*

# JIM EWAN

*During the war the railway was classed as a reserved occupation, it was of national importance so railway-men were not conscripted into the forces. When Jim Ewan was seventeen he wanted to be a dispatch rider, and even went for his medical but he'd have had to leave the railway and was afraid he might not get back in again.*

You had to be sixteen before you got started on the loco side and the minimum height was supposed to be five feet but I got in though I was an inch short. I worked with an undertaker as an apprentice joiner then went to Dundonald colliery till I was sixteen. In 1943 there was plenty of work on the railway and I began as a cleaner and worked my way through the grades - passed cleaner, fireman, passed fireman and finally driver. Passed cleaners did everything, labouring in the sheds, cleaning, fire raising and dropping, clearing ash pans; a passed fireman was one who was eligible for driving. He had the routes and everything in mind and could be called out by the foreman if they were stuck for a driver but even if you were an experienced driver you only got first year driver's rates. You never got extra for working overtime except for nightshift, you got time and a quarter for that. Drivers took a pride in their engines, and were cleaning and polishing all the time. Most drivers had a big lump of waste and cleaned as they went along.

*All spit and polish. Driver Andrew Wilson prepares his engine for visiting photographers Thornton August 1966*

Every engine had a brush, shovel and spray pipe. There was a tap fitted to the top of the injector and the footboards used to be white because the water from the boiler was red hot. You had to carry a gauge lamp so you could see the level of the water. If you had to leave your engine you sometimes had to come home by passenger train carrying your lamp and brush etc. Thornton didn't have the fast trains, the expresses, it was a mixed traffic depot. We went to Perth, Edinburgh, Glasgow and Montrose but most of it was local with passenger work round the coast to Crail, Anstruther, Newport and Dundee. It got to be we couldn't do change-overs with Glasgow men because the other drivers were on diesel and wouldn't take on steam.

Thornton was the last depot in Scotland to be working with steam. In the end they changed us over from steam to diesel in about a fortnight. Instructors came and stayed in the Station Hotel and in one weekend the engines were all sent up the bing road waiting to be scrapped. In later years we had to go to Leith to be trained in new engines. We were fortunate because we had a shot of both steam and diesel. We had DMUs - diesel multiple units, the sprinters have taken over from them - they were good when they were new but were run into the ground. The locos got so bad that we came out on strike to get them repaired and they built an examination shed. It was called the snake pit and the examiner had to check every nut and bolt and he could order repairs to be carried out.

Even diesel locos had their own peculiarities. One job we had was on the line coming up from the Dubbie where there was an S bend that came across the main road at Dysart .We'd manage twelve wagons but the gradient was steep and you'd give it full power with sparks flying – past the petrol depot with men filling up the tankers and going out to deliver. Nothing ever happened, I don't know how.  The diesels couldn't take the load, the wheels just birled. The steam locos had a coupled traction - a side rod coupled to a driving wheel but the diesels were individuals and one set of wheels would work and another wouldn't. They were small twelve to fifteen hundred horse power; later we got the two thousands. Steam engines weren't measured in horse power you went by tonnage and according to gradients, it was about three hundred and fifty tons for passenger trains depending on what was needed and the number of coaches. There were always more at busy times.

At holiday times the whole of Glasgow used to come here before they started going to Spain and there'd be a train every five to ten minutes. No-one got a day off and everyone was fully employed. You got all different kinds of locos, some we'd never seen before. Holidays gave you a shove up, relief drivers were always needed so you got extra turns. You needed so many turns before you could be appointed driver but you might be driving off and on for years before that happened. You had to wait till someone retired before you got promoted and the average length of service was fifty years.

*Loco 62475 Glen Bleasdale approaching Kirkcaldy. Goods shed on right, Steve Robb's 'office'*
*in foreground – a concrete box which replaced the wooden bothy*

## CONVERSATION PIECE -
## DAVID SKENE, GEORGE WATT AND WILLIAM MUNRO

*Whenever two or three railwaymen are gathered together, they are a bit like old married couples - they bicker amicably but interminably, share common memories and even finish each other's sentences. If there are more than two it's difficult for any other person to get a word in edgeways.*

I joined the railway in 1942 but before that I worked in the foundry at Leven, making wings for Hurricanes. Both railway and munition works were reserved occupations so I had to explain to the dole why I wanted to change from one job to another. I told them I wanted to make the railways my career so I got started at Thornton. I went for my medical the same day as John Matheson, he was older than me but because I started a week before him I was senior to him. If two people started on the same day, the older one got seniority, but we all started as cleaners and worked our way up. During the war, there were no materials but they scraped enough to clean an engine just to let me see what I should have been doing. One of my first jobs was as caller out. You went up the town in the morning to waken drivers for the early shift and if you missed one you got reported. The first time I was on call, I took the names off the roster sheets but the first person I tried to knock up was on holiday in London and I knocked up half the miners in Thornton that night. I was a stranger from Methil. The caller out was blamed for everything - if apples or strawberries were pinched, we got the blame.

A driver's job was different to the rest, there were no regular shifts and sometimes you wouldn't see a mate for months at a time. You had regular jobs and conditionals. You wouldn't know where you were going till you left the shed and the guard would come and tell you. Maybe you'd take coal some place or empties up to a colliery. Methil goods, Cupar and Glencraig were special jobs.

*Coal train from Redford*

Cardenden had four pits at that time - Glencraig, Minto, Brighills and Dundonald . There was a Glencraig pilot that worked all the pits. He would meet the train, take the empty wagons in and come out again with the full ones. Other trains, like the Cupar, leaving in the morning would be marshalled in the yard .You went to Lady bank, did a shunting job, took off some stuff. Road vans were taken into the shed to be unloaded, they carried stuff for shops in Ladybank, Cupar and Markinch. On the Methil line there was material for Buckhaven and

*Heavy aluminium trains climbing out of Inverkeithing towards the Forth Bridge*

Wemyss Castle as well as Methil. Lorries would be waiting to pick it up for delivery. The trains had names, the morning one to Townhill was called the Grocer, the later one was the Derby and the last one was the Scrap because it picked up all the odds and ends. Most of the coal was shipped from Methil but some still went from Burntisland and we carried powdered alum from the British Aluminium Works to Cawdor Yard in Glasgow. There were special restrictions on those trains. The wagons had to be kept a certain way for discharging the powder by compressed air and the outlet had to be on the right side for arrival at Fort William.

My first job, as the youngest hand, was messenger. At the beginning of the day shift I worked in the store with oil and so on, went to the station to bring materials and trimmed coal for the Glasgow. The train didn't have time to come down to the depot and because it used a lot of coal coming from Glasgow, I had to get up on the tender and push the coal forward so it was within reach of the fireman. The Glasgow men had a PNB, a personal needs break and the majority gave us a hand. When trains went to Glasgow and Edinburgh they had time to go to the depot for coal and water. Maintenance was usually done during the night. When engines came into the shed they were put in rotation according to the time they were going out, that was the shed men's duty. Maybe there'd be six rows of engines that had to be oiled, watered, coaled and cleaned. During the day engines came in and out continuously just to get coaled.

When we first started, promotion was pretty quick because there were a lot of coal workings. Thornton had built itself up into a big depot and it stayed that way for a lot of years. It declined as the coal industry did and

*Cameron Bridge Station with old DCL wagons and the water tank in foreground*

went down even more when the pits closed because it was mainly a freight depot, not too many passenger trains. Everything we did was local. There were a lot of depots then, three at Edinburgh, St Margarets, Haymarket and Dalry Road. When we started it was LNER, then after nationalisation we joined up with the LMS. We went to a lot of different places after that because we'd never worked LMS lines before. We had four sub-depots, at Methil, Anstruther, Ladybank and Burntisland. There was a passenger engine stationed at Anstruther and three sets of men. What happened was that the last passenger train from Edinburgh was left at Anstruther overnight and the first men out in the morning worked it back to Thornton. We did the goods trains to Anstruther and they took them on to St Andrews. You couldn't do the whole trip on your shift. If you delays - a seven hour job might take nine and a half hours - you got overtime but it wasn't from choice. You had to finish your train. If your shift went on too long, you got biscuits, they were like hard tack, to keep you going but the cost was kept off your pay. You were very lucky if you got home in your eight hours. You could be shunted to let passenger trains through or have problems with snow, or with the engine.

The promotion system was odd. On the traffic side you had men coming out of the signal boxes into the yard and they didn't know the first thing about the job. It wasn't their fault, it was the way the system worked but they had to rely on the men they were supposed to be supervising to keep them right. Signalmen were well up in the rules because they had to apply them more than anyone else. Once we got promoted, nobody tested us.

Guards knew how to marshall, they worked the pits, knew what traffic to take and leave behind. When they took coal to the docks at Methil sometimes they had to mix the coal, not for cargo but for the ship's bunkers. Three different types and quality of coal would be mixed and it was easy to get it wrong. One of the guards used to work just between Methil and Kirkland and one Saturday backshift about five o'clock, it was just getting dark but he didn't bother with a tail lamp. Unfortunately there was a lot of activity about Kirkland and they were late in getting in. Guards always carried a red flag so he stood in the rear wagon, waving his flag and lighting matches.

We were members of The Thornton Benevolent society begun by Donald Macaulay which covered an area from Aberdeen to Kings Cross. You received money if you were off sick. Willie Anderson known as Maternity Bill, was the local agent for The Railway Benevolent Fund and Convalescent Homes. If you saw a young chap chasing after him you knew his wife was pregnant. The fund faded out after superannuation and the Railway Pension Fund began. You had to be under forty to join but we older ones were allowed to pay extra contributions. Payment began to be made into the bank though some chose to continue the old way. If you were on night shift you could miss the pay because you had to go to Thornton to get it. The yard was a good way from the station. We cycled all the time - up to Thornton at all hours, even in snow and ice. Sometimes we got a lift on a train but there was nothing between midnight and six am. Men were reliable though they travelled from as far away as Pitlessie.

We finished up driving rail cars between Edinburgh and Kirkcaldy and Edinburgh and Cardenden. Promotion then was quicker. You did pilot to Auchmuty and Sinclairtown, short goods trips, conditionals, Aberdeen and spare. There was a great need for spare men especially in the morning to cover for men who were ill or had slept in. In summer there was a 'shove up' you did certain jobs while other men were on holiday or you could be sent to other depots and at the end of summer you were shoved back down again. We all got to be drivers and got to the top of the tree but firemen were stuck for a long time. They couldn't get promotion till someone died or retired. Things weren't so bad after nationalisation. I got to be driver only two years after passed fireman.

When it was steam working in the shed you were kind of separated but when diesel came in you had more contact. When we shifted to the new shed there was a big reduction in staff. With diesels, no preparation time was needed. You just went in and started it up, you just had to wait for air pressure. All the railcars were out of the shed by eight o'clock for the commuters to Edinburgh every half hour and once out, they were out for all day. If anything went wrong with a steam engine there were things you could do to get you back to the yard. If a diesel went wrong you shouted for help and prayed.

The run down was very quick. The 1984 miners' strike was the end - pits like Seafield never opened again. Longannet was the main job, three trains a day beginning at 1.55 in the morning. The semaphore signalling was changed over in one weekend. We were given a diagram. No driver was given training you just got told how it was going to work. The coloured lights were easier than the old signal system. They started on the Edinburgh Glasgow line first and we were involved at Winchburgh Junction so by the time it came here most drivers had some experience. We went to Leith for training to drive diesels. George was an instructor when the 350 Shunters came in and the Hunsletts. Drivers trained for a week.

# DAVID MCFARLANE

*David started on the railway in 1935 at the age of fourteen, beginning as an engine number taker and ending up as a driver. He loved every minute of his job and has many happy memories .These are just a few of them.*

My father was a shunter. He'd done different jobs on the railway, was a signalman at Methil West and a guard for a while. When I was ten I used to clean his bothy every Saturday morning, blackleading the grate and scrubbing and polishing. I remember in 1926 during the General Strike, my mother would go to a shop in Commercial Street in Methil and get her messages on credit. When I started on the railway I worked three shifts for two years at Kirklands Yard till someone realised I was too young to do night duty and I was shifted to Wemyss Castle. I applied for a job at Thornton and got sent to Dunfermline where I was to start at one minute past midnight on a Sunday. I had to beg for time off to go and find digs. You could be sent anywhere at a moment's notice and they weren't concerned how you got there. When I worked at Anstruther I had a fifteen mile cycle from Methil and, when I finally was given a permanent job at Thornton, I cycled eight miles there and back every day for nearly thirty years. I could have got a house there but I didn't want to move. The kids from Thornton had to go to Buckhaven High School at that time and they got the train at eight in the morning and didn't get back till five at night. So I kept on cycling. It wasn't too bad going but coming back against that east wind was terrible.

When the war began, I had to go for a medical and was offered the choice of navy or air force but like most railwaymen I was exempt from the armed services. I remember being at Falkland Road on the day of the first raid on the Forth and I had to go to Dundee on the Monday. I was twenty when the war started and was on steady nightshift at Anstruther. I had a carbide lamp and was stopped at the Caley corner because it was too bright. I think I was one of the first to be fined. I went to Cupar to be charged and was fined seven and six.

*Thornton Home Guard*

I was one of the first to join the Home Guard in Leven . They had an armoured train which was stationed at Thornton. It had a funny engine, they couldn't get steam, so instead of square bashing and night watching I volunteered to be the fireman. I had to cycle to Thornton for that as well. I got a lift on a motor bike once with a bloke who was a dispatch rider but it didn't have a pillion. My foot was resting on the exhaust and the sole of my boot was near burnt through. We used to go down to the Links between Largo and Kilconquhar to fire shells. One Home Guard man had a gun and he used it to shoot hares and rabbits.

In 1967 or thereabout, the Railwaymen's Travel Club hired a plane to go to Rimini - fifteen days for twenty six pounds. That was my first holiday abroad but the next year about thirteen of us went to Moscow for the May Day parade in Red Square. We had special passes to get into the square. We went through Sovscot in Glasgow. Our free passes took us to Brest on the Polish Russian border and then the carriages had to be lifted on to other wheels because the gauge was different . We had a twenty four hour journey from Warsaw to Moscow. After that we went back another six times for Burns Suppers. We were treated like lords and stayed in what was supposed to be the biggest hotel in the world. Bill Keith the butcher from Kirkcaldy did the catering and we took everything with us - haggis, potatoes, turnips and whisky.

There were half day trips you could go on and we visited a school - School Number Six it was called and the bairns there recited Burns poems in Scots to us. It was marvellous to hear them speaking our language which is more than most of our own bairns can do. One boy asked if Russian was taught in our schools and we were ashamed to say it wasn't. We went to see the Hall of Economic Achievements. One exhibition was about farming and they bred rabbits for their fur to make hats and gloves and the meat was fed to hospital patients because they believed it helped to cure them quickly. Another was the Space Achievement Centre and there were twelve gold statues, one to represent each Soviet Republic. We went to see the changing of the guard at Lenin's tomb at ten o'clock at night.

I've been to Czechoslovakia several times and made friends with people who came to stay with us in Methil. We met one man, a high heid yin in the police, at Edinburgh and persuaded the driver to let him sit in the cab going over the Forth Bridge. This was after the diesels came in of course. Once though, I was going for my train and this man was running thinking he was late. I told him I was the driver and the train couldn't go without me so there was no rush. He was Bobby Pagan an organist who had been performing in Edinburgh and he asked if he could cross the bridge on the footplate. Afterwards he sent us a letter of thanks and four tickets for his show, for me and the fireman and our wives. He dedicated a piece of music to us during the performance.

We had a job at Thornton where you took the train down to Anstruther and the men from there took it on to St Andrews. The engine used to stay there overnight but after the war started they couldn't have engines sitting doing nothing so my fireman and I were sent down to fetch it. We went down on the passenger train and I saw a golf ball lying on the side of the track so on the road back I let the fireman drive, got him to slow down and I picked the ball up. A week or so later there was a bit in the Sunday Post from a man complaining that an engine driver had stolen his golf ball. He must have seen us stop, but it wasn't his ball.

One day we had a train of coal from the Wellesley pit going to Kirklands and the fireman was driving. The other pilot was in front of us with another train . There's a turn and a bridge at the bottom of the yard. The signal was off but as we turned the corner the fireman started to yell. The train in front had started to shove back because he had gone on to the wrong road and we smashed into him. We had nine buffer locks and some wagons off the rails. I got the blame of course because I was supposed to be driving. The next day the station master asked if I'd written my report but I said I didn't want to write lies. I told him he was lucky I wasn't driving because I'd have been going at a harder lick and anyway, we had almost double the number of wagons we were supposed to have. If I was going to be blamed, I'd make sure it didn't happen again, everything would be done by the book. One Friday afternoon when we were trying to get finished up we had a train of one hundred and seventeen empty wagons coming from Methil. I never heard any more about it.

People used to throw coins off the Forth Bridge for luck but they didn't all go into the water. They were repairing the bridge once and we were on caution - five miles an hour maximum speed, that's just walking pace. On the side of the line the pennies were easy to pick up but between the lines it was grooved so it was difficult to get back up on to the engine again. During one of my money gathering trips I found the plaque on the side of the gold rivet put in by the Prince of Wales when the bridge was opened.

# THE SIGNAL MEN'S STORY

## ANDREW HUTCHISON

*Andrew was born and brought up in Thornton, worked on the railway for forty seven and a half years, thirty three of them as a signalman, and loved every minute of it. Though he didn't come from a railway family both his sons have followed in his footsteps and are now engine drivers, one working with the GNER, the other with SCOTRAIL.*

My father was a miner and he always said he'd murder us rather than see us go down the pit. He had three brothers killed in the pit, two at Balgonie before I was born, the third at Rothes Colliery. He was the only man to be killed there, though another man who worked for the Cementation Company was killed when they were sinking the pit. My first job was keeping a record of all trains passing the signal box and I had to learn all the bell signals. There were various classes of signal box. Thornton West was a one man box but it was a special class so had a register boy. Thornton Station had two men plus a book marker. It was huge, about sixty to seventy feet long with one hundred and one levers so you had to run from on end of the frame to the other. It had a stove at each end but was still cold because of the wind coming up through the bottom of the box. The wires from the box connected to the signals and the rodding went to the points.

*Thornton Station signal box, looking north.*

I did my National Service from 1953 -55 in the Black Watch, did basic training in Perth then was posted to Dortmund and Dusseldorf. When I got back I was given a temporary summer job at Cardenden signalbox then went permanent to Dalgety Box, just about where the station is now. It was two shifted, afternoon and night shift and two of us worked it. The other man stayed in Anstruther and we had an old bike we kept at Aberdour Station. If I was starting work, I'd pick up the bike at Aberdour, cycle across the fields and my opposite number would meet me half way and cycle back to the station on it. There was supposed to be an offi cial hand over but the Inspector probably knew what went on and turned a blind eye to it. We had to go to the farm for water, we got it in a big enamel can. One afternoon I went to the box, got the can and arrived back at the box at two minutes past three. The inspector was there and complained about me being two minutes late. Most main line boxes worked three shifts but as things got quieter a lot stopped night shift - Markinch for one, Dysart and possibly the Randolph as well. When Thornton opened first it was busy on all three shifts. I've seen trains standing right from the yard to Thornton North. I worked thirty three years in signal boxes and when the boxes closed I put in for a supervisor's job at Thornton. They opened a carriage cleaning plant and I worked there for about five years. There were supervisors for different departments, train crew, yard and carriage cleaning. They did away with the plant after six years and I got a job as platform supervisor at Haymarket Station covering some one who was on long term sick leave. I was never appointed officially and after six months I was sent a redundancy notice. I never said anything and one day the roster clerk phoned me up to ask me to work my rest days the following week. I told him it would be hard because I'd have finished up by then. It went from the roster clerk to the traffic manager and then to the operations manager and I was asked to stay on and was given the job permanently.

*Goods train passing Dalgetty Box, 1951*

I stayed a couple of years until a job came up at Perth - I wanted to move back into my own grade - and I worked constant six nights a week for five years till I applied for redundancy. I didn't want to go on working till I was sixty five, I knew too many who had and didn't last more than a month or two after.

I always loved my job and we used to have a lot of fun in the boxes and some hair - raising things happened as well. I was on call once and was asked to check on a signalman because there was a passenger train standing at Thornton West and they couldn't contact him to clear it through the section. The man was in the big chair and I knew he wasn't dead because he was still breathing but I shook him and shouted at him and couldn't rouse him. I phoned and asked them to get a doctor because he was unconscious and I put the train through. I was standing at the window watching it go past - we had to do that in case any doors were open or anything else was wrong - when he jumped up and asked what I was doing there. He said he was just exhausted, he'd been up all night unwell but the doctor came and took him home in his car and he never came back to work again.

I was working in Perth in 1962, I'd got what they called compensatory promotion. They couldn't get staff because signal boxes were closing and no-one wanted to take a job that wouldn't last. Friarton box was a class one box, open seven days so you got Sunday work. When they were relaying the Moncrieff Tunnel going into Perth, I was early shift one Sunday morning. The overnight sleeping trains were coming in from Euston on a single line and the ballast was on the dead road. The men were working there with the engineers. I was talking to the flag man out of the cabin window and the points were set for the fast to come flying through. I saw the headlights of the sleeper coming through the end of the tunnel and at the same time there were three red lights coming towards me on the dead road. My hair was standing on end. There was nothing I could do about it. The fast train flashed past and the red lights came out of the tunnel and over the detonators - we always put down detonators to protect the road - the train stopped and the guard came to speak to me. I went to town on him 'It's alright' he said, 'we kent the fast was there. We were bringing the men out for their piece.' I sent for the Chief Inspector, they'd no business to do that. I nearly had a heart attack, but they just got a caution.

On another occasion I was at Markinch. We had a local goods working Leuchars to Thornton and it was in front of the up fast and between me and Thornton North. It was past Lochmuir and I was doing a shunt with a whisky train when I saw the fast had gone through the home signal. I didn't have time to put down detonators so just grabbed a red flag and stuck it out of the window. The train was showing no sign of stopping so I sent the signal for a runaway train to Thornton because as far as I knew the goods train was still in my section. He gave me the all clear to say the train had passed him and I pulled the signal to give the train clearance but the driver had pulled on his emergency brakes and stopped an engine and carriage length past the signal.

He sent his second man back to see me but I went to meet him and told him to forget it because no harm had been done. The next day the district inspector came to ask what had happened. I told him it was a fairy story, nothing had happened but two of the railway bosses from Glasgow were on the train and they reported it when they got back. Probably there was a lot of tea and coffee spilt in the dining car when the emergency brakes went on. I was charged for not reporting it but when I went up to the inquiry I had a union rep with me and he told me the driver had already been punished - he'd been reduced to second man and they couldn't punish both of us. It was his fault no mine but I got cautioned for not reporting it. The driver thanked me for trying to cover up for him. We often did that if no harm was done especially if it was a freight train that was involved. If damage was done it was out of your hands because we had to get the Signal and Telegraph linesmen to repair it. There used to be two separate units, one for points another for telegraph but they amalgamated. We were supposed to report any damage. Another time I

*The old North British railway gantry which controlled the exit from the Leven Branch to Thornton Station, the carriage sidings and the line round to the west.*

was on late shift at Lochmuir. The sleeper passed about nine forty five and one of the doors was open, so the line had to be inspected. I was finished my shift by that time but I was asked to stay on and help. They found a man not far from the Lochmuir box. They reckoned he was drunk and had opened the door to go to the toilet and when the train struck the curve he fell out. The way he fell, all the fingers on one hand were cut off. The doctor came and had to walk about a mile along the track. He never bandaged the man's hand or anything - it was all swollen but was sealed where the train had gone over it - just said that apart from being drunk there didn't seem to be much wrong with him. We found out later that he had a fractured skull and had brain damage. He was a master fisherman and was on his way from Aberdeen to his home in Newcastle.

I was asked to meet the ambulance on the main road and bring it down through the fields. There was a big dip down by the line and I said he'd have difficulty getting out if he went right down, but he went down anyway and after we'd put the man in the ambulance it took several of us pushing to get it going. The police were there too and I asked them if they were going to take his fingers away because if they turned up later people might think the rest of the body must be around somewhere. The police said no, but days later were back trying to find them. Too late then , the crows would have gone off with them. They were looking for papers as well and the track walkers were asked to keep a lookout but they never turned up.

The box was about three quarters of a mile from Kirkforthar, there used to be cattle in the fields there and we used to cycle down the farm track to the box. On nightshift, the rats would come in beside you, when it was quiet you'd hear them coming up through the frame. There were dozens of boxes in Fife and on that stretch of line you had Falkland Road, Kettlebridge, Markinch, all the Thornton boxes, Redford, Clunybridge, Cardenden, Lumphinnans and Lochgelly. It's all worked from Edinburgh now. You read sometimes of cattle on the line and trains being delayed for hours. That never used to happen, nor were civvie police involved. Railway police weren't involved either unless animals were killed. They don't have a P-Way squad now, every length had its own squad and if there was a problem you just phoned the ganger to come and clear the line. Plus you cautioned all the trains through the section, you didn't stop them. The phones in the signal boxes were push button so half a dozen of us could carry on a conversation at the same time. You enjoyed the company and the comradeship.

*Since leaving the railway, Andy has concentrated on his garden raising thousand of seedlings each year, some of which are sold for charity and he has what he describes as 'a drawerful of medals and trophies' won at flower shows for dahlias, fuchsias, carrots and onions as well as others he can't remember.*

*Thornton Station signal box home signals. Left to Leven, right to Dundee*

# JOHN PHILP

*John Philp worked as a signalman for fifty years and his proud boast is that in all those years he never lost a single day's pay from illness or absence.*

My father was a fireman but he switched to being a guard. If your father was on the railway you were more or less guaranteed a job, so after working as a clerk at de la Rue's paper mill, I went to Thornton as a train register boy or apprentice signalman. At the junction there was a train at least every five minutes and each had to be recorded. You had to start at the bottom, and rules and regulations were paramount. You had to know the railwaymen's handbook inside out. All the signal boxes were graded with the biggest ones being 'specials'. After five years I went to Lochgelly as porter signalman and eventually worked my way up to special class signalman and from there to district relief which meant I covered a section from the Forth Bridge to Burntisland and from Thornton to Stirling. I did everything on the railway bar driving a train. I've taken horses from Edinburgh to various places in Fife . There used to be racing at Kilconquhar in the thirties.

*B1 afternoon train from Crail arriving in Thornton.*
*Thornton's biggest signal box in background.*

There were one hundred and eight engines running full time at Thornton then and over a thousand people working there. The ganger had to check the line every week unless there was subsidence, when he had to do it every day. Single lines to Methil and Leven to St Andrews were worked by tablet. The station went steady for twenty four hours a day, steam was paramount, a pall of smoke hung over everything and coal littered the place. It went from Wemyss, Bowhill and so on to the docks at Methil and Burntisland for export. There were three places for repairing wooden wagons but then they changed to steel and from eight to ten tons they went to twenty ton wagons and that did away with the private wagons belonging to the coal companies. For a time the herring trade had a good run, from Anstruther and Crail but that didn't last long. Everything went by rail from cows to coffins.

Summer evening excursions went to Balloch with a sail on the loch for half a crown and trips went to Portobello baths. Sunday trips went as far as Fort William and in June there were Sunday School trips. In all those years, the railway from the Forth Bridge to Burntisland carried billions of passengers with not one fatal accident. Diesel finished coal on the railways and it turned the community right round. There had always been full employment in Thornton, either on the railway or in one of its subsidiaries - workshops, joiners, electricians and so on. Women worked as clerkesses and during the war as engine cleaners and in signal boxes. I used to train them but they weren't in the big boxes. The men who worked them had gone through all the grades.

You didn't have to pay taxes for unemployment benefit. You couldn't be paid off and had permanent employment unless you got into trouble with the law but if you got into trouble with the law or were caught pinching you were dismissed instantly. There was a Railwaymen's Benevolent Society which was begun by a driver called Macaulay and went all over the country. You got three free travel passes a year and unlimited travel at a third of the normal cost.

As well as working in all the signal boxes in Fife and Kinross, I had to test crossings once a month with the linesmen and examined men who were going through the grades. For a while college graduates were being taken on as station masters and I had to teach them the rules and regulations. I checked all the colliery lines and there were plenty of them. The Fife Jewel coal from the Wemyss and Rosie pits went to the royal household. It was the very best. For a ton of coal you got only half a bucket of ash.

Trains ran on time and the crews were properly trained then. If you went through a signal you were off the footplate. During the war, shunters worked for eight hours with a twenty minute break in the blackout, with hand lamps in rain and sleet. When the war stopped the railway sent a doctor with numbers on a little book and if you couldn't tell the numbers and colours, you failed the eyesight test. It was called the Ishihara test. You had a medical examination every five years between the ages of forty five and sixty and yearly after that.

---

**British Railways** Scottish Region

Movements Manager
Operating Officer (East)
Waverley Station, Edinburgh.

Tel. 031-556 24 77 Ext. 333

D.R. Signalman J. Philp,
THORNTON

y/r
o/r O2/176-701                    5 December, 1972

Dear Mr. Philp,

PLAIN TRACK DERAILMENT : THORNTON 4 10 72 : B65/1,
HYBAR 492227

On behalf of B.R.B. I should like to express thanks
for your prompt action in warning the driver of
Freight Trip B65/1 that all was not well with his
train as it passed Thornton Station Signalbox on
October 4 1972.  Your alert response to the emergency
was instrumental in avoiding further damage when one
vehicle was already derailed and your action is highly
commended.

I shall be pleased if you will accept my own personal
thanks for your vigilance on this occasion.

Yours sincerely,

for OPERATING OFFICER (EAST)

---

We didn't have full uniforms. To begin with we only got a waistcoat with gold buttons. Station masters got nap coats and I got one because there was single line working at Ballater and if anything went wrong with the tablet system I had to go there. The station masters at Glasgow, Edinburgh and Ballater got top hats. Men came from Ballater and from Glencoe and Mallaig to be trained. I could have got promotion but didn't want to move. I stuck to special class boxes and nobody could tell me what to do. Funny things happened at Thornton. A shell from an aeroplane buried itself in the signalbox and that caused a row because a deputation from Leuchars came to inspect it. They said it couldn't happen. Once a train split at the top of the hill, went on its side and shut the junction for a day. If there was a derailment you went to Edinburgh to the District Supervisor who made an enquiry and apportioned blame. In October 1957 I was highly commended for preventing an accident. A train with forty coal wagons was going across the Junction at Thornton and a wagon in the centre came off the road and fell on its side. I saw it happen and got the driver to stop.

*No reward for vigilance,*
*just a thank you letter.*

# THE CLERK'S STORY

## TOM SHERRY

*Tom comes from a mining family who moved from Lanarkshire to Fife after the General Strike in 1926. When he left school Tom worked as a cine -operator until he was called up four days before Christmas in 1944. He did an eighteen week course of physical development, specially designed for small men and those who were tall and gangly, and put on a pound every week. After serving at Chichester, Woking and Southend, he was sent to Sierra Leone on the Highland Princess and visited Casablanca where all the ships had been scuttled. From there West African troops who had been in Burma were taken down the coast. These men had been taken from the bush, fed, clothed and, in the opinion of the governing department, trained to kill and were returning home to plan revolution and insurrection.*

When I got back home I started in Nairns as a linoleum tester, but passed my railway exam and got taken on as a booking clerk at Kirkcaldy Station. This didn't work out because I had difficulty adding up columns of figures and if I was three pence out, I made it up out of my own money. I was transferred to the parcels office and then to Markinch before starting at Thornton. One of my jobs was paying out the wages. We began at twelve on a Thursday and finished at nine.

After two years I got a scholarship to go to the Catholic Workers College in Oxford. It's called Plater College now and was designed for people who had reached a certain level of education but couldn't afford to go to University. British Rail would not give me the time off. Later I found a signalman was given leave but I lost three years service and when I came back there was no job for me. I studied principles of economics, social theory and philosophy and economic history and theory with the Catholic slant on the topics of the day. The social teaching of the Catholic Church is similar to Communism, the only difference is the way they go about it. Communism would get rid of everything, nationalise everything without compensation, while the church believed that was tantamount to stealing. I had a grant from Fife Council and Oxford was wonderful, especially in the summer. There was cricket in the parks, you got in free and I saw most of the cricketing heroes of the day. At the end of the first year, I scraped through but I made a mess of my finals and didn't answer the questions properly so came home with nothing to show for two years intensive study.

*View from Station Bridge Thornton showing  left to right – carriage sidings, both south  and north main lines to Edinburgh. and Dundee with Leven platform in centre and booking office in foreground*

I began labouring, working from eight in the morning to ten thirty at night, putting in a new pit head at the Francis Colliery, then did a spell with DCL before getting back my old job at Thornton. I did summer relief at Dundee, Dunfermline and Thornton before being made permanent relief. I had to go round the various depots arranging holiday relief rosters and they all had different ways of working. At Dunfermline there were no Saturdays off. Thornton was one in three off and Dundee one in four.

After the locomotive office was merged with the area manager's office, I was made redundant and went to work in Kirkcaldy dealing mainly with medical cases, arranging medical examinations and fitting people into jobs they could do. In 1970 I became roster clerk at Thornton for the loco men. It could be quite a stressful job - in Dunfermline for example the ballast, the first job of the day, went to the most senior driver and fireman; in Dundee all senior men were on sleeper and day passenger jobs. Drivers had to know the road, every signal in the section. Most difficulties were when drivers were on holiday - we had to make lists of drivers, firemen, pilots, engine prepare men. Once I listed a man who was dead and buried . At Thornton holiday rosters had to be posted a week in advance so the LDC ( Local Departmental Committee of NUR/ASLEF) could scrutinise them. Men always had to work at Thornton because the place was so cold that engines had to be kept working. Christmas was always the worst time because of the two holidays following on each other. People complained about being rostered on Christmas and New Year's Day but someone had to do it. One man always volunteered to work Christmas Day because he wanted time off to go to Moscow for Burns Night. Thornton had one big exception to the rule. Nobody worked on New Year's Day twice running.

In 1963, six special trains were planned to go to Glasgow for the European Cup Final and I had to find twelve sets of men to man them. On the Wednesday before the match, three of the trains were cancelled. When diesels came in I had to go to Dundee because the chief clerk there was off sick. During the changeover, ten men at a time were being taken to Perth to train on the rail cars and that left little leeway for organising the remaining men. At the end of the training period, I was congratulated on a job well done.

*After retiring in 1988, Tom worked for a time with the Youth Training Service, labouring and driving, and finished up doing local history recordings. One was made with George Russell, a railway inspector who had been a passenger guard in 1953. He told of a train carrying East Fife supporters to Easter Road in Edinburgh which was full before it left Methil and had to pick up passengers at East Wemyss, Buckhaven and Wemyss Castle. At Thornton three carriages and an engine had to be added to cope with the crowds there.*

*Thornton yard with ticket office. Golf Club hut on left*

# THE SHUNTER'S STORY

## ARCHIE SCOTT

*Archie was born in Glencraig and brought up in Lochore. His father and brother were both miners and he watched them coming home covered in dirt and coal dust and decided he'd rather do anything else. He worked on a farm before starting on the railway as a greaser at the age of fourteen . At sixteen he had an accident which kept him off work for three years. Working with a pilot coming from the Aitken pit, he slipped, the engine went over his foot and he lost all the toes on his right foot.*

When I started again I went to the wagon shops at Thornton, that was in 1947 and in 1950 I got an examiner's job at Townhill - wheel tapping, examining doors and so on - and did light repairs in the yard. After that I worked in Kelty for twelve years before getting a shunter's job at Thornton. Kelty yard was being close down and I was offered a relief job but that would have meant travelling to Markinch and Methil and I didn't want to do that because I had no transport.

Est. 82—12/38  5,000 pads of 250

## LONDON & NORTH EASTERN RAILWAY.

B. 1154

M. E. .........................DEPARTMENT     To The Manager,

Burntisland, ...........STATION     Labour Exchange,

9th February, .........19 42     Lochgelly.

OUR REFERENCE     TELEPHONE NO.     YOUR REFERENCE

F.42/10.     Vacancies - Greasers.
-------------

    There is a vacancy for a greaser at Kelty, the rate of pay is 16/- plus 5/6 war wage, per week.
    Will you please issue a green card to Alex Scott, 30 Ballingry Road, Lochore who is an applicant for the job.

*Archie's first job*

The new yard was up and going then and there were jobs you had to progress through. At the hump yard you started at one end as shunter, then went on to top end shunter then cutter. When trains came in you checked every wagon and uncoupled the ones going off to different places. Next step up was operating the hump system. The hump is where the wagons go out of the sidings over the hump into the roads. There were thirty six roads and they were all controlled mechanically and had their own braking system which kept wagons from flying down the hill. In some yards you had what was called a brake stick and you had to hand brake them. When the hump closed I got made a chargeman in the yard. We made up different trains for different areas, Glasgow, Edinburgh and so on. There was a scrap train in the morning that went all round the branches from Inverkeithing to Burntisland calling at all the stations on the way. Traffic for certain companies had to be put together, like coal for gas works at Dundee and Perth. Cards were put on every wagon showing where it was coming from and going to, what it contained, type of coal etc and the tonnage. When I was on the wheel tapping we put 'not to go' cards on some wagons and they went to the repair lie at Kelty and Townhill. We had to do light repairs during the early shift, putting on springs. bottoms of axle boxes and fixing doors. You had to go round every train that came in. In the early days you got a lot of grease boxes overheating. Now its all ball bearings, no oil needed .Shunting was a lot easier with diesels than with steam engines. I was at Kelty when they came in and the merry go round wagons took a lot of coal from Lassodie to Dalkeith and across the water to the power stations over there. One of the early ones had a door open, one of the latches hadn't been put in right and we had to go underneath to repair it. We had to stop because it was too dangerous, under a loaded wagon with not much room trying to jack it up. We got many a soaking under the old wooden wagons when they were filled with wet coal, we'd come out looking like miners. We had no problems with steel wagons, the doors on the old ones were hard to close. There were wagons with cattle, fruit and vegetables but it all changed to road transport, even the whisky. There used to be trains taking whisky from Markinch. There was a pilot at Haigs that took the wagons to Thornton.

I wanted to go to the loco department but it was a bit of a struggle with transport. You weren't allowed to do shifts till you were sixteen. I got an offer of a job at Dunfermline and the afternoon shift was two till ten but the last bus left at nine thirty. Anyway they started me at Townhill and let me go half an hour early.

When I started again after my accident it took me two years to get back to the job I wanted to do. It was a seven day week and when you had a day off you had to work two shifts in one day to make up for it. Most of the work was with coal trains, there were four engines at Kelty working the pits, bringing coal to the yards. All the pits, the Mary at Lochore, the Aitken, Lindsay and Lassodie, were on braes off the main line. You could only bring twelve wagons out of the Aitken at one time but from the Lindsay you could do thirty or forty. You had to watch there was a brake on the wagons. One ran away, struck the buffer ends and knocked down the signal for coming off Dunfermline Upper. We worked Blairadam brick works as well and I remember once a train came down from Lassodie and went right through the crossing gates. At Townhill, I used to

take the mail, the paper work to go to Burntisland, from our bothy. There was a branch line to Townhill Power Station, and to Muircockhall and Lathalmond which was just at the back of the bothy. I was just about to cross the line when I looked up and saw a brake van hurtling towards me. Luckily the points were lying from where it had come from and it hit the buffers. It had just come out of the shop after repairs. Another time a train ran away from Lumphinnans Central and the signalman didn't bother to send a warning because he was sure the hill would stop it but it came right over the hill. I had to run and shout to the boys on the pilot to get out because they were going to get hit. Luckily they managed to escape but the yard was shut for about twenty four hours. The train was old wooden wagons, one full one split in two and an empty one didn't have a scratch on it. When accidents happened reports had to be filled in. I never regretted going on the railway. I enjoyed my job and there was great cameraderie among the men.

*Left to right – Alex McIntosh, George Galloway, John Cooper, Andrew Bunyan*

# RAILWAY WOMEN

If you lived in Thornton, it was said, you were either a miner's wife or child or a railwayman's wife or child. To be an engine driver or fireman's wife was no easy task. Everything revolved round the railway. Isabel Grant, whose husband Andrew worked for forty five years as an engine driver, remembers her puzzlement when her husband-to-be turned up for their first date carrying a small attache case.  It held his working clothes because he was on constant night shift at Burntisland. 'He used to take me to the dancing,' she said ,'and get his pals to take me home again. No matter what time of day or night you went down the street, you'd meet men either coming or going from their work. I think there were dozens of different shifts. They could start at two in the morning or in the afternoon or any other odd time. You just got used to it and children learned to keep quiet when their father was in bed during the day. Sometimes we hardly saw each other from one week's end to another and  much of our social life was a solo activity.' One result of the irregular shift and eating patterns was that  a number of loco men, including Isabel's husband, died young from stomach cancer . She reckoned it was caused, at least in part, by lack of regular  proper meals plus the inhalation of smoke from steam engines.

*Although women had been employed as clerical staff since Victorian times, during the Second World War, women worked on the railway doing jobs that had been strictly for men before then.  Aldra Stocks  worked at Thornton for  thirteen years.*

I worked in the  Markinch Co-op for about a year after I left school, but  went to the railway in 1942. This was a railway village, my father was a fitter and turner  and it seemed the right thing to do. I worked as a telephone operator for a while doing back shift and day shift. We were  just fourteen, too young to do night work but there was only one operator on each shift. It seems funny now such young girls doing that job - in winter going down there at six o'clock in the morning and on back shift it was after ten when you got home. It was a seven day a week job and we only got one Sunday off in three months. The conditions were terrible. There were rats living in the coal heaps and I remember once I lifted a lump of coal and flung it. It hit a rat, not the one I was aiming at , but never let on when I got cheered. I made an awful blunder once. The Control was at Burntisland and the man on Control that day was Sandy Kershaw. He phoned and told me there was an engine at Lochgelly with a slack tyre. I thought he was pulling my leg but an hour later he phoned again wanting to know why no-one had turned up to fix it.

I moved on to the general office at the Motive Power Depot, the first woman to be permanently employed at a depot in Scotland. It was all men before the war, of course, but office staff were not exempt so they were conscripted and they didn't all come back. The girls that took their place were classed as temporary workers. It was easy enough to get office staff but you couldn't pick up an engine driver at the Labour Exchange. They had to be trained up from cleaner to fireman and driver and it took years for some of them to be made up. There were one or two girls  on the clerical staff and I did shorthand and typing and general office work. I wouldn't join the Railway Clerks Union, but chose the NUR because they took people from all grades. Other unions like ASLEF took only engineers and firemen.

When it was the LNER,  there was a running foreman and one telephone operator  running the office .When British Rail took over they added an assistant running foreman, a time keeper, roster clerk and telephone attendant but they were doing the same job that two people were doing  before. I used to wonder how the railways could pay with the ridiculous amounts of staff they were taking on.

*Thornton Station staff around 1890 included five ladies*

*Cluny end of Thornton yard with water towers in the background*

# THE TELEPHONE OPERATOR'S STORY

## GRACE DUNCAN

*Grace Duncan started work on the railway as a telephone operator when she was fourteen. She was born in Glasgow where her father worked as an engine boiler builder at the famous Cowlairs yard. At a time of high unemployment the yard went on short time working, then he was paid off and moved to Thornton and a job as a boiler smith, mending rather than making engine boilers.*

When we came to Thornton first we lodged with a mining family and I remember the man coming in with his moleskin jacket and trousers and the carbide lamp still in his cap. It was wonderful for my parents to get a house with a garden because in Glasgow we lived in a tenement with a toilet shared by three or four families. I remember we had a sink in the window and my father made a special chair. I was tied into it with a big woolly scarf so I could look out of the window. I loved hearing my father talking about making the big new engines. When they were completed, they went to the docks to be shipped out to foreign countries. The big factory gates would be opened and everybody would be standing outside with their flags, watching the big gleaming monster coming out. A lot of engines went abroad.

After my father started work at Thornton I used to go up to the shed to see him in the blacksmith's shop and I'd climb up into the cab of the engine. When one was brought in for repair, the fire would be dropped in the wet pit and the engine towed away. The minute you looked into the firebox you could feel the heat where the fireman had been shovelling coal just a few hours before. My father's cap would be on the back of his head, a sweat rag round his neck and perspiration running down his face. He'd buy leather by the yard for soling his boot because the hot metal burned right through them, and would sit with the last between his knees, cutting out and hammering the new soles. Because I started work when I was only fourteen, I wasn't allowed to do night shift, so just did day and back shift. The office was connected to the shed and I worked alongside the

*Grace Duncan on left with Ethel Dick and Bess Blyth far right*
*Among the men are Jimmy Davidson and Andrew Dewar*

shed driver and the supervisor. There were five phones - one that took calls from outside, for example if drivers could not get in to work; one for signalmen, all the signal boxes were on that line; one for Thornton Station; one for Burntisland Control and the last for the yard supervisor. Outside the office was a huge board with a list of all the trains going out. Normal trains went out at the same time every day, conditionals times you got from Control. Drivers would ask where they were going and you told them what yard to go to and what to pick up. The signal man at the Weighs yard phoned the most. That was the box going out of the yard and he wanted to know the number of each engine and where it was going so he could change the points to put it on the right line rather than have the engine driver slow down to tell him.

The yards phoned to ask which jobs engines were on  so they would know the tonnage to give. We were kept quite busy. There were huge books about two foot tall and eighteen inches wide and you had to keep a record of every train going in and out, the times, the engine, load etc. Another smaller book was for passenger trains. I sat nearest the fire on a high stool with my book. The supervisor wrote up everything that happened, rather like a sister in a hospital. Before he finished his shift he had to tell the one taking over absolutely everything that happened - if and why he'd used spare men, if anything happened to an engine and so on.

*Engine in wheel drop, axle boxes taken off for repair*

If a goods engine was ten minutes late in getting out it didn't matter too much. I remember one Saturday I saw men off when I was on backshift and when I started Sunday day shift they still weren't back in the yard. They'd come back looking like miners, especially if they'd been on the Glasgow run. Sometimes they'd have 'a fire in their eye', grit or dust from cinders or flying sparks. My father was in the ambulance section and he had a special gadget for getting these out and I got one too and became quite expert. We used to get coded messages from the telegraph office at the station, not real code, just the message would say one thing and you knew it meant something else. This was for ammunition and troop trains and the royal train. The shed driver had to keep all the other engines in the shed at those times so the trains could have a clear run through with no delays.

The conditions people worked in would never be tolerated today. Engines came into the coaling plant, got watered then went to the wet pit and the fire droppers cleaned the fire. Even though the doors and windows were shut you could feel the sulphur in the back of your throat because the hot cinders went into the wet pit and all the steam and ash came up. The fire droppers looked more like men in a mill shop or factory, grey with dust. From there the engines went round and put into the right lie and they were like horses all lined up for the start of the race. I had to work Saturdays and most Sundays, there were no rest days then. My last job before the end of the day was to clean out the ashes and make sure the fire was going well - that's where we boiled the kettle for piece time - for the next shift coming in. There wasn't much doing on Saturday nights, very few trains so I would start tidying up about half past six and the supervisor would let me away early. Women didn't normally do that job but it was war time and Aldra Wishart and I started at the same time, doing shift about. We wore trousers and Aldra's mother made us coat overalls out of blackout material. It was the only stuff you could get without coupons, everything was rationed. Anything else we'd never have kept clean with the smoke and dust from outside.

*The wet ash pit in winter*

I worked there for about four years till I got married - to a railwayman of course. Dave joined the railway in 1944. Before that he worked at the Co-operative but he became an engine driver. His father was yard foreman at Methil so I've been surrounded by railwaymen all my days. I loved my job and everyone was very good to me. Drivers would bring cakes that their wives had put in their piece boxes for me. Particularly on a Sunday when there was hardly anything doing, two of the supervisors would take me out on the engine. Maybe the shed driver would be busy and I'd give them a message, say a breakdown or something and the engine had come into the coaling plant. Rather than go through the shed they'd take it round the office so it could be dealt with right away. Sometimes they'd let me open the throttle and one day Jim Graham took me down to the turntable. They say it's easy to operate but I couldn't get it to go round so he told me to drive while he did the turning. I went too fast when I came off and he had to run to catch up. Once I was taken on an engine which had been made ready for a changeover for the Glasgow train up to the station while my grandparents were arriving there for a holiday. There have been times since when I would have liked to put on a pair of dungarees and get up on the foot plate again.

# THE ENGINE FITTER'S STORY

## LILLIAN CANT

*One of a family of five girls, Lillian was born and brought up in Aberdeen. After she left school she spent a summer developing photographs, working a twelve hour day, then went to Watt and Grants outfitting work-room, mostly making and repairing corsets. When that work dwindled she was taken on in the baby depart-ment. The family had no rail connections and Lillian's introduction to the railways came about because she failed her medical for the forces. Going from selling baby linen to repairing engines was, as she said, really going from the sublime to the ridiculous but she was lucky compared to her two sisters who ended up in munitions factories in Birmingham.*

Some of us who didn't pass for the services were sent on an eight week training course to become engine fit-ters. I was nearly thirty at the time because it wasn't till well into the war that they started calling up older women. Jean was ten years older than me and I remember coming to Thornton in January 1942. We left Ab-erdeen at nine in the morning and had to change at Dundee. We took the first train to Thornton but it was a slow train and went all the way round the coast and when we reached Thornton, nobody was there to meet us. Eventually a girl arrived but she was from Burntisland and didn't know her way about Thornton. We had to ask directions to our digs in Strathore Road and hump our heavy cases all the way there. Luckily the weather wasn't too bad but I thought that day that Thornton was the last place God had made. We couldn't even wait for a cup of tea but had to go and see the shed master and started work the next morning.

I really enjoyed my time on the railway, there was only once that one man was kind of nasty. We were pulling a big nut off the front of an engine. There was a big key on the nut and maybe half a dozen men pulling on the rope. I was told to stand back but the man said, 'This is your job, get on the end of that rope' but the oth-ers wouldn't hear of it. We were very lucky, I believe the girls that went to Dundee had a terrible time of it. We did mostly light work, facing valves, fixing boxes for big ends and sometimes worked inside the engines. We knew them inside out, did practically everything except the heavy lifting. The leading fitter could have driven us, but he didn't. I worked for a while doing running repairs, any wee job that needed to be done when the engines were in to get coaled and watered. We worked outside. On the engine's smoke boxes there were a lot of nuts to take off the cylinder. You tied the first on to a string then threaded the rest on in order. They had to go back the right way because sometimes the heat went for the threads. Then there were the injectors and whistle valves, men didn't like that job because it was light handed work. In the wheel drop, axle boxes had to be replaced and we used pulleys to lift the wheels.

There were three or four women fitters and to begin with we were just labourers to the fitters - there were six or eight on day shift and one or two on nights, but we ended up as engine examiners, tapping the wheels with a big heavy hammer. We were bonny looking dearies with boiler suits and scarves round our heads and not a scrap of hair to be seen. The engines were coming in and out continually some getting their periodical check ups others needing big ends relined or just minor jobs. I worked a lot with Mr Edmondstone, the shedmaster and his two sons. He got an awful scare one night. We were working on an engine and the connecting rod had been pulled up. The rope slipped and the rod bumped my head as it hit the crossbar but I wasn't hurt. We used to all collect in the smiddy because it was nice and warm and the coppersmith aye had a fire going as well. Sometimes the men weren't fussy what they said and I didn't always understand what they were on about but I laughed along with them and we always got on well.

We were really lucky with our digs and there was always something to do. We borrowed bikes and went for runs, there was the NUR and Association Guilds and the Social club. Hardly a week went by without some-thing on, dances, dominoes and whist. people were friendly too, and invited us to their houses. An Aberdeen family introduced themselves because the wife's sister got my old job at Watt and Grants. I never went back to Aberdeen but never regretted coming to Thornton, I got married in 1944 and left the railway the next year before my daughter Lillian was born. Dave came from a mining family but he left the pits and worked as a surfaceman for a while before becoming a fitter. My sons didn't become railwaymen but are both involved in the model railway club and worked up at the Lochty Branch when The Union Of South Africa was there.

# THE TELEGRAPH OPERATOR'S STORY

## BETTY FORRESTER

I started work as an operator in the telegraph office at Thornton Junction in the spring of 1944 after being a Morse instructor in the A.T.S. The method of transmission was entirely different from 'key sent' Morse which sounded in dots and dashes. The railway telegraph instruments relayed in 'clicks', two different sounding clicks per machine, - one click represented the dot, the other the dash. The area of Thornton transmission was approximately sixty miles in radius and Thornton was one of a series of relay stations. It received the surrounding stations and signal boxes and forwarded messages to Perth, Glasgow and Edinburgh. By 1944 the signal box men used telephones to communicate but in England, Morse was still in use.

The telegraph office was a room off the main office and had six telegraph instruments, five wall phones to signal boxes and a Post Office phone used for sending telegrams. The public could use this office for sending telegrams - there was a 'bowl' which opened on to a platform - and the price was then ten words for one shilling, the town and area counting as one word.

*Some of the mass of sidings at Thornton*

Jimmy from Dundee, whose place I was taking, explained my duties and gave me the information about sending telegrams. The forms were kept in a drawer along with 2/6 worth of change. 'But don't worry,' Jimmy said, 'I've been her for five years and no-one has sent one yet.'

Not long after, I was working on my own when I heard a constant tapping that puzzled me, and there at the 'bowl' was a crowd of soldiers wanting to send telegrams and their train was on the point of leaving. It was wartime, they had landed by boat at Methil and wanted to let their families know. They had no small money, they'd have got paid when they landed, I suppose, and I had only two shillings and sixpence. Eventually an NCO paid the lot. I wonder if he ever got the money back.

Mornings in the telegraph office were always busy and every instrument would be in use, all chattering at once because whosoever was sending on any given instrument had full use of the machine and the message could be read in any office which held that instrument line. When an operator had a message for Thornton, he repeatedly signalled Thornton's call 'TY' so I would acknowledge and write down the message. As well as those to be relayed, for the main office and information for the inspector on duty, there were hooks in the office to hold messages for different railwaymen such as the plumber and electrician etc. and these men would look into the office during the day, checking their hook.

Women had taken over many railwaymen's jobs at that time to free them for the forces. Mainly they worked in the ticket offices and as carriage cleaners and guards. I remember one time a railwayman came laughing into the office. 'It's like a battlefield out there, 'he said, 'women fainting all over the place.' Luggage had been grouped to go in the guards van of an approaching train and a child's pram had rolled off the platform on to the line and of course some of the women staff thought the baby was in it. It wasn't funny but *he* thought so - a couple of women fainted.

Thornton Junction was always extremely busy, the platforms often were thronged. Passengers changed there for the coast. I can't remember if there was a canopy over the platform. There was maintenance staff for the buildings as well as the rolling stock and I was always amazed at the many different jobs men did on the railway. For instance, there were signal boxes at numerous points and the 'station box' was just at the end of the platform. The man had to watch each train that passed, checking that all door handles were in the 'shut' position and that there was a tail lamp on the last carriage. If there wasn't, a carriage could be missing. Twice I received a message for the station inspector saying, 'No tail lamp on....... train,' (the dots denote a time, not an oath)

I had no knowledge of women doing signal box jobs or shunting. I think they were reserved for men who would not be allowed to join the armed forces. Shunting was a dangerous job if the men did not obey the safety rules. They were supposed to remain away from approaching carriages and not link up till the vehicle completely stopped but of course if they were in a hurry, they'd use the pole sooner than safety allowed and even stand between the buffers.

Complete honesty was also expected. The slightest act of stealing - a lump of coal or a fish off a piled high fish box - meant instant dismissal.

The wagon and engine sheds were manned twenty four hours a day. The cleaning of stock was done there, engines prepared for scheduled journeys and extra heads of steam in case of breakdowns. I'm not sure of the time it took to prepare an engine before it could be used but I know the firebox had to be cleaned out and the water heated to a certain degree before the engine would move. It took a few hours. The sheds also had inspectors. They normally wore bowler hats. I understood they were to protect their heads.

The women wore uniforms similar to the men, some, especially the platform staff wore trousers. I don't remember what all the platform buildings were. There was a waiting room where we could use the toilet and a bothy for the staff to take their breaks. Our heating was a round stove, coal fed, in the middle of the floor and a bucket of coke stood beside it. It was dangerous to overstock it because it could get red hot and the whole place was built of wood.

I was always amazed at the conglomeration of railway lines at Thornton Junction. They seemed to be a great intertwining mass with points all over the place. The main lines leading off to the coast were crossed and recrossed by others to the sidings. Some of the officials had office huts within the rails and if I had a message for any of the men I stood on the platform and yelled till they heard me and came across the lines to see what I wanted. *Nothing* would have tempted me off that platform.

*The Barry, Ostlere, Shepherd linoleum factory, Kirkcaldy*

*Kirkcaldy goods yard showing the volume of traffic. In the foreground are the steam pipes joining two parts of Barrie's buildings which were on both sides of the line.*

*Inverkeithing Pilot at Ferryhills*

*The Abbot has a new number but note the old LNER tender*

*WD 2. 80, 90220, at Burntisland with aluminium wagons. Built for the War department, and a bad steamer she was christened 'Ice Cold Kate'*

*Coal sidings being lifted at Lumphinnans Central*

*Shunt engine for Thornton shed, Jim Watson, driver*

*Inside the shed: the inspection pit and the barrow used to carry brake blocks: they were too heavy to carry*

*Shunting at Lumphinnans with Lochgelly Golf Course on right*

*WD ballast train en route from Cowdenbeath to Lumphinnans loaded with concrete sleepers; remains of Lumphinnans Number 11 Pit and Lumphinnans Pond*

*Thornton Coaling Plant 1944 –line up includes David Mackie (driver) Steve Drummond,*
*Willie(Darkie) Young, Harry Brown, Robert Dewar*

*Thornton Steam depot 1965 . Back row l-r –Harry Brown, D Laing,*
*J. Reid, Hugh Docherty*
*Front row – J. Fyfe, G. Duncan, Tam Graham, Abe Reid, J Pattison.*

*90049 at Thornton North End yard with shunting engine*
*Cattle market refreshment rooms on right*

*Thornton Station with passenger shelter on left*

57

*Glasgow Transport Museum. Archie Scott and Andrew Grant with Glen Douglas which Andrew used to drive.*

*David Duncan with Union of South Africa*

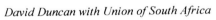

*Glencraig Junction controlled lines from four collieries*

*Carriage sidings and station at Thornton looking south from the footbridge*

*Thornton's 1933 sheds and coaling plant, known as the cenotaph, taken from the top of the water tank*

*The Lucy Ashton at Thornton Station*

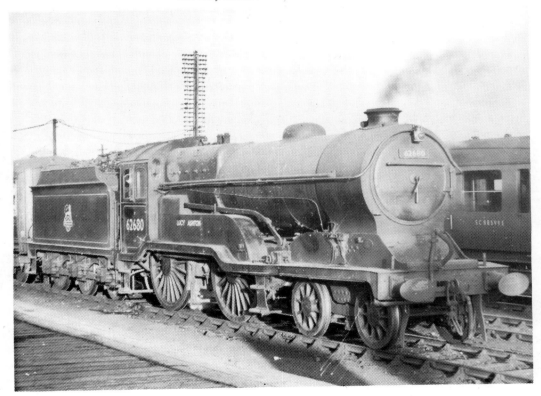

# THORNTON'S FAMOUS MEN

Wherever big events are taking place in the world, there are sure to be Scotsmen there. One Scot, a Mr Black whose father owned Tulliebreck Farm near Thornton, apparently wrote the American Declaration Of Independence in 1776, having been chosen for the quality of his handwriting. The connection was discovered by a Glenrothes man, who saw the original document in Philadelphia. during a visit sometime in the thirties.

Another Fife man, James Wilson, whose family farmed Carskerdo in the parish of Ceres, emigrated to America in 1765 after his father's death and settled in  Philadelphia. He achieved an outstanding reputation as a lawyer and was elected to Congress in 1774  and in 1789 was appointed Assistant justice of the US Supreme Court. He signed the  declaration document on behalf of the State of Pennsylvania and though the draft of the Declaration of Independence was written by Thomas Jefferson, it is believed that he used a theory which Wilson had developed and published as a pamphlet in 1768. Wilson's story is told in a book published in 1910 which  claimed that one hundred and eight  years after his death, Wilson was given an official state funeral. His remains were removed from North Carolina to Pennsylvania and he was re-interred close to his friend and colleague Benjamin Franklin.

David Hatton, or Flutorum as he came to be known, was born in Dunfermline in 1874. He was an eccentric whose inventions included  the Chamber Flutorum from which he got his nickname. This was a musical instrument made from two German flutes with a set of bellows attached. He also claimed to have invented a device which would throw shovelfuls of coal on the fire at six in the morning, have a kettle boiling for his breakfast by  six thirty and then pull the clothes off his bed to get him up. In 1812, Hatton went to Perth where a prison had been built to hold French prisoners  - the Napoleonic Wars were being fought in Europe at this time - and was amazed at their ingenuity. To augment their pitiful rations, the men made little articles, including toys to sell. one which caught Hatton's eye, was a model of a house with a wheel attached to the gable

end, which was driven by a mouse. He bought the toy and the mouse and began a series of experiments to develop a treadmill operated by mice which could be used to pin thread. He made massive mathematical comparisons and believed that his mouse mills would compare favourably with the cost of steam power. He planned to lease the Auld Kirk in Dunfermline which he reckoned could hold ten thousand of his mouse mills. Unfortunately no-one would invest in his scheme and its only use was for exhibitions and raising money for charity.

In 1829 Hatton moved to Thornton and became a grocer and innkeeper. His tavern was distinguished by a set of whale's jaw bones. He had a museum which held ali his inventions, and wrote pamphlets and songs which he sold, the proceeds going to charity. He also sold snuff which probably came from a snuff mill at  Leslie where Robert Kirk, a Kirkcaldy tobacconist, began making snuff at the Sparrow Mill in 1805. Another of Hatton's money making schemes involved him lying in the coffin he  had made for himself,  being dressed in grave clothes and holding the bottle of whisky which he claimed he'd take with him to the next world. People paid a penny to see him, but  this scheme ended when someone closed the coffin lid and  nailed it down. He never got in it again during his lifetime. He died aged sixty seven in 1851 and is buried in Dysart.

# JOHN CAMERON

When John Cameron died as the result of a road accident at the age of eighty three, newspaper reports mourned the passing of one of Thornton's 'most distinguished and respected residents of the century.'

Born in Glasgow in 1881 and trained as an engineer and fitter, John finished his apprenticeship in the Atlas Works in Springburn in 1901 and moved to Thornton in 1905. He was a leading member of the Independent Labour Party and was Parish Councillor for the area from 1910 to 1919. With the reorganisation of local government he represented Thornton on Fife County Council and was County Councillor for Markinch North from 1919 till he retired in 1945. He was the first Labour Convenor of any committee and later went on to become Chairman of Fife County Council Police Committee, of Kirkcaldy District licensing Court and of many local Hospital Boards.

The time spent in public service was made possible by his working constant night shift. There were no high salaries in local government in those days. It was regarded as almost a voluntary occupation. Even in 1945 the allowance for loss of a day's work was only fifteen shillings (75p), subsistence for four hours 1/9 (8p) and for eight hours the equivalent of less than eighteen pence. John Cameron's aim at all times was to improve the health and well-being of the people of Fife and with his colleagues he fought for and helped to achieve acceptance for the necessity of better social conditions. His enthusiasm for work in the community became a yardstick for those who followed in his footsteps. After his retirement in 1946, he continued to serve his local community and was 'a man who was selfless in his sacrifice and who by his example, inspired others.'

## AL MURRAY

Alastair Murray was an undefeated Scottish champion weightlifter, a British record holder and an Olympic coach, whose career began in a wooden gym in his father's back garden in Brown Crescent, Thornton. His father, grandfather an uncle and cousin were all engine drivers and another uncle was a boilermaker's assistant. Al's first introduction to weight lifting was by a railway fireman, George Galloway. Al worked for Tullis Russell and John Law, one of the mill managers, provided the gym. The firm gave him a replacement when the first gym was destroyed in a freak storm. In a newspaper article in 1994, in which he was photographed receiving an award from Arnold Schwarzenneger, Murray paid tribute to Sir David Russell, chairman of Tullis Russell, and also to Harry K Brown of Thornton who presented the gym with its first set of international barbells. In those days the barbells cost the equivalent of a small car.

During the war, Al became a Sergeant Major Instructor in the Army Physical Corps and afterwards trained as a remedial gymnast at Bridge of Earn Hospital. He went on to organise physical culture shows in the Adam Smith Hall. A commentator at the 1948 Olympics, he was appointed the first ever British and Olympic coach, a position he held for twenty five years. He and his wife moved to London and his City Gym became famous because of the research work they did with the Medical and Sports Council, investigating methods of training for very unfit adults and for cardiac patients. Al switched from weight lifting to general fitness training and developed special remedial exercises known as the Murray Method. He coached at many world championships, at Olympic and Commonwealth Games and set up coaching schemes in many countries. Famous members of his gym, which became a victim of the IRA Baltic Exchange bombing in 1992, included Bernard Miles and Laurence Olivier.

# JOHN ALLAN

*John Allan with Jean Mackie, Provost of Dunfermline*

*(Reproduced by kind permission of The Dunfermline Press)*

John Allan's family were railway men for four generations and between them they practised many of the rail-way trades - porter, lengthman, fireman, driver, guard, signal fitter, examiner, wagon inspector and even plumber and covered the whole period of steam. The railway system was very much a family affair. Sons fol-lowed fathers in the service and often the only way to get a start was to have one's father or a close relative on the railway. It was not well paid, but was steady work and security was very important.

John's father was a passenger guard and was involved in transferring goods from the train to the ferry-boat from Granton to Burntisland. The crossing of the Forth was done in all kinds of weather in winter and sum-mer and he caught a severe chill which turned to permanent bronchitis. Following the opening of the Forth Railway Bridge in 1890, the Allans moved from Edinburgh to Dundee, to Sinclairtown and then to Buck-haven. After a short spell as passenger guard at Dundee, Mr Allan was given the job of goods shed foreman at Sinclairtown and later he transferred to Methil as a carriage and wagon examiner.

This was in 1894. The following year, at the age of eleven, John started work firing a steam crane at the building of No.2 dock at Methil. Leaving school at lunch-time, he started on the night-shift at the docks at six o'clock the same day. Part of his firing job was to fill a sack with coal from a wagon and carry it some thirty yards to the steam crane. In his twelve hour shift he would transport about a half a ton of coal. After a year there, permission was given to his father to start a wagon-greaser because of the rapidly increasing traffic at the docks. "I was given that job'" said Allan, "and so became the first greaser to be employed at Methil

Docks". In 1897 he became an engine-cleaner at Thornton Junction. This was a constant night shift job. It also involved going around the district "knocking-up" drivers and firemen between midnight and six a.m. for early morning duties.

In 1899 John passed out as a fireman, and when he was appointed engine driver in November 1906, he returned to Methil Docks as shunting pilot, putting West Fife coal wagons to the hoists for the loading of ships. He was also on the Leven Dock pilot when that dock was filled in and when the Kirkland Yard was developed and when the line was doubled between Leven and Thornton to meet the large increase in coal shipments. He was promoted to Thornton in 1914 as banking pilot driver, and later still, to the locomotive goods working, then to the local passenger trains and then on to spare link trains whenever required. In 1920 he became a locomotive inspector, stationed at Thornton, his district extending from Dundee to Stirling and from Perth to Edinburgh. Later the area was increased to take in Aberdeen and he moved to Dunfermline to be more centrally placed.

In 1937 he was promoted chief inspector in charge of the Scottish Area. For two years this meant his being stationed in Glasgow. He transferred to Edinburgh when the department was set up there and returned to Burntisland in 1940. After a strenuous period during the war, he retired in 1946 after some 50 years of railway service. His membership of the Union, The Amalgamated Society of Railway Servants, which later became the National Union of Railwaymen, began in 1899. He was a member of the National Executive Committee from 1916 to 1918, and over thirty years was, at various times, Secretary of the Methil Branch and of Thornton No.1 and No.2 Branches. John was also involved with convalescent homes and was a member of the railway section of the St Andrews Ambulance Association. Railwaymen were encouraged to join the Ambulance Section and Thornton had a particularly outstanding team, winning local and national trophies. As an incentive, the LNER granted an additional free pass to those attending the class.

*North British Railway engine Glen Gloy. Driver Tommy Thomson, Inspector John Allan,*
*Shift Foreman William Sandison, Shed Foreman J. Ellis*

But the railway did not take up John's whole attention. Throughout his life, education was one of his greatest concerns. In 1918, he joined the Fife Education Authority representing Thornton. Leven and Markinch, and this association was to last twenty five years. He was a co-opted member of Fife Council Education Committee for three years when it took over responsibility for education in 1929 and from 1945 to 1955 was convenor of Fife Further Education Committee. Appointed to the Board of Governors of the then Heriot Watt College in 1922, John was still associated with it when it became a university, and was later awarded an Honorary Master of Letters degree. He spent three years on the Board of Dundee Technical College and was a member of The Advisory Council of Lauder College. He was elected to Dunfermline Town Council in 1933, six years after coming to live there and remained a permanent figure in local politics till his death. He held many convenorships and represented the local authority on outside bodies including the Carnegie Dunfermline Trust. He was Honorary Treasurer for nine years, a Bailie, Chief Magistrate and held the office of Provost from 1955 to 1958. In 1960, he was elected Citizen of the Year and in 1962 was awarded the Freedom of the City and admitted as an Honorary Burgess in appreciation of twenty nine years public service.

But his public commitments went back further than twenty nine years. He was involved in the Co-operative Movement from 1906 and remained a member till his death and was heavily involved in the political life of Thornton. A branch of the Independent labour party was formed in the Public hall there on December 4th, 1916 and at the age of thirty three, he was its first president. Two years later he was indirectly subjected to criticism by a motion from Lewis Wilson that 'members of the ILP should vote in accordance with their principles.' The Thornton branch of the National Union of Railwaymen had invited Mr Whitelaw, chairman of the North British Railway to chair an Orphan Fund concert. Allen was told by Sir George Sharp's father that 'You can't run with the hare and hunt with the hounds.' The motion wasn't carried.

John Allan was a member of the Forth Road Bridge Joint Board, took part in such widely varying activities as Fire Prevention, Golf, Amateur Operatic and Dramatic Societies. His name lives on, not only in the memories of his railway friends and colleagues but in a more permanent fashion. Allan Crescent in Dunfermline bears his name, as did part of the old Lauder College Complex.

*Thornton Railway Ambulance team*
*John Allan with, among others, James Allan, David Thomson, T. Crawford. Station master and wife.*

# AIR COMMODORE SIR ARCHIBALD LYTTLE WINSKILL
## KCVO. CBE. DFC *AE

Archibald Winskill left Carlisle Grammar School in 1934, and having been thwarted by the slump from taking up a career in the Merchant Service, he joined the London North Eastern Railway Company , with the object of obtaining a Traffic Apprenticeship, the doorway to the top echelons of the company. This entailed working at stations and offices within easy reach of Edinburgh in order to attend classes on a number of railway subjects including Law. In 1937, he joined the RAF Voluntary Reserve  as a student pilot and started training at weekends at Scone aerodrome. By the time he arrived to work at Cardenden railway station around 1938, he had graduated from the Tiger Moth aircraft to the Hawker Hart which was quite a 'hot rod' for those days. and was drifting further away from railway engines and closer to aviation. He sometimes 'buzzed' Cardenden, which was quite illegal and  gained an odd ball reputation of the 'laddie from the station who flies'. It was rare to see an aircraft in those days. His memories include the chief railway clerk whose hospitality was exceptional and a Station Master who reported him to Head Office for being three and a halfpence down in the till after a particularly busy excursion train had left for Edinburgh. He had particularly fond memories of miners and these were reinforced when he was shot down in France in 1941. Miners risked death to help him escape and he returned to the UK via Spain and Gibraltar.

*Archie Winskill (second right) with William Young (Darkie), shed foreman on left, at Cardenden Station*

After his escape and return to the U.K. Archie resumed flying Spitfires with Fighter Command and served in North Africa. Before the end of hostilities he had been awarded the DFC and bar. After peace was declared he chose to remain in the RAF and had a very distinguished career holding several important posts. He was at various times Air Adviser to the Belgian Government. Commanding Officer at RAF Turnhouse and RAF Duxford, Group Captain Operations Germany, Air Attache Paris, Director Public Relations MOD, and for the last fourteen years of his service, Captain of the Queen's Flight. During his service in the peacetime RAF, he rose to the rank of Air Commodore. In 1960 he received the CBE, in 1978 was made a Freeman of the City of London and he was knighted in 1980. He is a graduate of the Army Staff College, the Joint Services Staff College and the College of Air Warfare.  After retiring from the RAF, Sir Archie became Extra Equerry to the Queen.

## SIR GEORGE SHARP

*Sir George Sharp was an engine driver, like his father and brother, but, unlike most of his compatriots, he left the railway and followed another - and extremely successful - career. He stood as a local councillor for many years and in a list of appointments eventually became convenor of Fife County Council, Fife Regional Council, Chairman of Glenrothes Development Corporation, a director of Grampian Television, Managing Director of Municipal Mutual Insurance, a member of Girobank Scotland and a member of the Scottish Development Agency. Between 1945 and his retirement from public service, he was involved with more than twenty committees, boards and commissions and his entry in* **Who's Who** *ran to several column inches. There was no danger, however, of him 'getting above himself', as he put it. His colleagues in the Thornton Railwaymen's Group kept his feet firmly on the ground. In fact,* '**Thornton Boy Makes Good'** *was suggested as a suitable title for this piece but it was said with tongue in cheek, the casual words hiding the real admiration and pride the rail men felt in their colleague's achievement. In the same manner he was subjected to gentle irony about his short term of service - only about twenty six years or so - but he saw himself first and foremost as a railwayman.*

I worked on the railway from the age of sixteen to forty two. I joined in 1935 as a telephone attendant and worked my way up to engine driver. I was Chairman of the Associated Branch ASLEF for fifteen years and also of the Local Departmental Committee. It was a great industry and if there had been the same opportunities then as there are now a great number of men would have been in more academic positions. There was a strict discipline and great loyalty.

In 1962, at the time of the Beeching proposals, I applied for a job as Railway Area Welfare Officer in Glasgow and was chosen from two hundred and thirty eight applicants. Willie Nicol Baird, the Divisional Manager of the Scottish Gas Board, had heard me speak at a meeting in the Adam Smith Halls and when he was told I was leaving Fife, he offered me a job. I'd been on the Council since about 1945 and with the offer of the job was the promise that I could remain a Councillor. I went to the Gas Board as a Public Relations Officer. On reflection, this was a remarkable decision yet paved the way for what has been regarded by many as a successful career. I was Chairman of the Water and Drainage Committee and later of the Finance Committee. In this year 2000, the rates are going up by five per cent. In 1967, during my time in office, rates were dramatically reduced by three shillings and three pence in the pound. I became convenor of Fife County Council, the second last President of the Association of County Councils and the first president of COSLA.

From 1969, I fought against the Wheatley Commission's plan for Fife to be split, and it was something of a miracle that we defeated the government on 20th February, 1973 by thirteen votes to ten. Ranged against us was a line up of past and present Scottish Secretaries - Gordon Campbell, George Younger, Michael Noble, Willie Ross. On our side were John Smith, Alex Eadie, Jim Sillars, Dick Mabon and others including Adam Hunter, and Sir John Gilmour. The local papers, in particular The Courier were very supportive. In 1978, I was invited by Bruce Millan, the then Secretary of State, to become Chairman of Glenrothes Development Corporation and I held that post for eight and three quarter years. To be asked to succeed Ronnie Taylor was a great honour.

Thornton was a thriving place then. I represented the area for thirty three years and never once had a case of eviction in the village. That meant I was really able to concentrate on being a councillor and didn't have to worry about sorting out affairs of people in financial difficulties. There was a degree of continuity of employment, Thornton had been prosperous for many years, the local economy was buoyant and the village demonstrated a degree of responsibility unparalleled in any other working class area in Fife. In the aftermath of war, it was anticipated that Fife would be the expanding coal field in the whole of Scotland.

*Balgonie Colliery , closed in 1960*

People were being transferred from Lanarkshire. In 1952 there were over twenty two thousand miners in Fife. The collapse of the industry was disastrous. I can remember going to canvass and people telling me they could no longer believe in the continuity of employment in Fife. The Rothes Pit was the last development planned by the Fife Coal Company before its demise, the last thing done by private industry. I attended when the first sod was cut by Augustus Carlow, the Chairman of Fife Coal Company on the Saturday prior to the coal industry being nationalised the following Sunday. Local miners knew it was sunk in the wrong place, it should have been further east, and they were proved correct. Glenrothes was built to accommodate the new miners it was expected to employ. Its logo is Ex Terra Vis - out of the earth comes strength. My former Latin teacher, Big Bill Reid, said it should have been Ex Terra Aqua. In spite of the Rothes fiasco, Seafield was hailed as a guaranteed success because it had the Rothes and Wemyss coal seams, but unfortunately these seams were almost perpendicular under the Forth. The only pit now is at Longannet.
I still stay in the street where I was born. At that time all but one of the sixteen houses in Rose Terrace and Thistle Terrace were occupied by railwaymen. Miners and railmen were very much politically orientated, very left wing, and from 1935 the area was represented by Willie Gallagher. I was asked to stand as a Communist member in 1945 and won in a three cornered fight. I wasn't keen to join the Council, I'd hoped to carve a niche for myself in the union but Thornton wasn't a big depot, you needed to be in Edinburgh or Glasgow to be effective. I left the party in 1951, I'd become disillusioned because they underwrote and slavishly supported every policy that Russia carried out. Then there was the invasion of Czechoslovakia and Hungary, contrary to the socialist philosophy that was being propagated. In the thirties when I joined, there was the Spanish Civil War and Mussolini was moving into Ethiopia. In my early days among the newspapers I read were Lansbury's

*Labour Weekly* and the *Reynold News*. I subscribed to the Left Book Club published by Gollancz at half a crown a month. Publications included Edgar Snow's *Red Star Over China,* R. Palme Dutt's *India Today* and *The Socialist Sixth of The World* by Hewlett Johnson, the Dean of Canterbury. One of the best books I read was *Between Two Wars* by 'Vigilantes,' Konnie Lilliacus, who became MP for Manchester Gorton. He had been an employee in the League of Nations and had seen the duplicity that was going on between Britain and France following a policy of appeasement against Germany. Hoare and Laval, the ultimate French traitor, agreed to the Anglo/German Naval Treaty allowing Germany to equal Britain's naval strength with disastrous consequences in the 1939 - 45 war.

In 1969, I was awarded an OBE and a Knighthood in 1976. Few people have had the good fortune I've had in my career and life. I have enjoyed the unswerving loyalty of my native village and area from 1945 to 1978. On one occasion eighteen years went by without an election. As Dick Mabon humorously said, 'George, the electors in your area can't read or write. 'That support has enabled me to be involved in a wide range of activities at local, national and European level. I've witnessed a social transformation in Fife. The street in which I was born and still stay no longer has a Poorhouse. As Chairman of the Water and Drainage Committee, I pushed the Regional Water Scheme in East Fife and the indignity of dry closets in schools and houses was eliminated. The miners 'raws' have been replaced and because of the driving force of people, miners and railwaymen like Izatt, Allan, Flint and Devlin, Fife the Kingdom blazed a trail in education unsurpassed in Scotland's local authority scene. As John Sneddon, known as 'Honest John' said, 'Nothing is too good educationally for our bairns.' Now in our midst and on the fringes of Thornton, we see the new town of Glenrothes, the administrative capital of Fife, which survived a number of crises in its early years. In the year 2000, the political and economic barometer appears 'set fair.' To have fought to preserve the kingdom has been a great reward but the friendship I've enjoyed at local, national and international level is something I treasure.

*Glenfinnan 9149, renumbered 2467. Driver James Hughes , Fireman David Lees . Hughes had four sons –*
*James ,Andrew and Tom, engine drivers and Willie, steam raiser - and grandsons on the railway.*
*Hughes named his house Glenfinnan when he bought it in the 1930s*

# ACCIDENTS

Accidents were mercifully rare. John Philp, who worked for over fifty years between Burntisland and Inverkeithing, took pride in the fact that in all that time and with billions of passengers being carried, there was not one single fatality on that line. In October 1957 John was highly commended for preventing an accident.

*Repair work after an accident at Thornton Yard*

There were accidents, of course, the first in 1848, not long after the line opened. Several passengers were hurt at the Tay terminus when a train ran into the end of the platform. In another incident the flange of one of the engine's wheels gave way, derailing it but the engine couplings snapped so the carriages stayed on the rails. Again several passengers were hurt and two died later. A letter to *The Fifeshire Journal* in 1848 suggested that train drivers should have a cap with a ribbon tied under his chin and with a cord attached that passed through every carriage the length of the train. This could be tugged in an emergency. Another letter in 1851 complained that 'On leaving Kirkcaldy station, guards are in the habit of checking passenger tickets by passing from carriage to carriage while the train is in motion.' nothing unusual in that, you might think, but there were no corridors in these trains and the guards were going along the *outside* of the train 'grasping handrails and leaning in at carriage windows.'

'I feel confident,' the writer went on, 'there is no passenger of sense who would not willingly forego a few moments of time rather than have his feelings harrowed by the fear of every moment hearing the death shriek of some of these men beneath the wheels of the impetuous train.'

In 1865, about sixty passengers in a Dunfermline train were injured when it ran into a stationary goods train south of Cowdenbeath station. The derailed wagons damaged a wooden waiting room which minutes before had been filled with passengers awaiting the arrival of their train. The Tay Bridge disaster is well enough documented not to need repeating. More recently, in March 1954, the Aberdeen Kings Cross express began slipping inside North Queensferry tunnel. There was a very steep gradient between Inverkeithing and the Forth Bridge, which often caused difficulties . The engine stopped and ran back over catch points and three coaches were derailed, blocking both lines. The following year, in May 1955, an engine overturned and derailed four coaches. The firemen and two unauthorised passengers on the footplate were killed and forty two people were injured.

There were less serious mishaps of course. Dave Mackie tells of his grandfather's very narrow escape. As an old man he worked the carriage pilot at Thornton. At the south end of the station, at the rail crossing in front of the signal box, going off duty to sign off at the engine sheds, his mind must have been on something else other than looking ahead, and the Glasgow passenger train came round the corner off the Dunfermline branch line. He was knocked face down between the rails and the train passed over him. When he was examined later by the doctor, all that was wrong was that he had a very bad gash across his back, and he had a scar till the day he died.

In August 1966, four railway men were injured and several others had narrow escapes when a diesel freight train with thirty four wagons collided with a coach rail car in a siding at Thornton. The diesel engine ploughed into the rear coach, telescoping it and throwing it into the air. A shunter, Magnus Matthewson had a miraculous escape. He was uncoupling coaches on the rail car when the accident happened and was thrown to

*Opening of new Thornton shed.*

the ground. He could do nothing as the coaches rolled above him and when he finally crawled out, realised that the engine of the goods train had come to rest above his head. Another person to escape injury was Isabella Mitchell, a cleaner, who was just about to get into one of the passenger coaches. There was a tremendous bang and the next thing she remembered was scrambling across the line with bits of railway carriage falling around her. Both drivers of the diesel and the locomotive driver and firemen required hospital treatment but were not seriously injured.

Nowadays we have become used to hearing leaves on the line as an excuse for train delays and people tend not to take it seriously but as Andrew Henderson explained they could be a driving hazard. The diesel wheels did not have the same grip on the rails as the steam engines, especially if the layer of leaves was thick and wet.

'I've run away before with hitting leaves, especially from Cumbernauld coming down to Greenhill Lower where there's a steep gradient and bends. I couldn't do a thing about it, because with a diesel, if the brake locks, it's like you've got square wheels. With steam engines you had three brakes, steam, vacuum and tender

*Lochty Branch 1947. Fireman Jim Ewan, Driver Alexander Adams*

*Fighting a losing battle with enormous drifts*

so you could control the train better. I was praying all the way down that I'd get the distant signal because I was going on to a main line, but it was against me. Luckily the signal man realised what had happened and switched every thing to give me a clear road. Steam engines were safer. It was the fireman's job to control the tender and that controlled the train. There were no brakes on the wagons only in the engine and guards van but if you started to slip on a gradient you could put the steam brake on in notches so it slowed you down gradually. Wet leaves are no joke. Neither is wet snow.'

Snow caused a lot of problems. George Watt tells what happened when he got snowed up on the Lochty Branch .'There was a bit of a gully and a train got stuck, We were sent up with two engines and a snow plough and the snow was packed hard. We'd draw back, charge into the snow and get stuck and the surface men had to use shovels to free us. I was walking along the gully with a traffic inspector and a surface man told us to keep to the poles because there were cut outs. The inspector paid no attention and disappeared up to his chest in the snow. They had a terrible job getting him out and he was soaked to the skin. We wanted him to go into the guards van to dry off but he insisted on staying in the engine to dry by the fire. But we were going back tender first and the cold air was freezing him. Another time we got stuck and Jock Braid the inspector managed to get a lift to go for help. He was never coming back and we found out later he'd gone home and had his tea.'

On another occasion, engines sent to clear snow ripped up the track and closed the line more effectively than the snow had done. During the terrible winter of 1947 a huge snow plough was hitched in front of three engines from Thornton to clear the drifts. All went well till near Mawcarse, near the county boundary between Perth and Kinross, where the drifts were so tightly packed that the small wheels of the plough were lifted off the rails but the impetus kept the engines running into Mawcarse Junction. The plough ripped up the rails and sleepers and the engines fell over onto their sides. By a miracle, no-one was hurt. A team under the direction of Chief Inspector David Steele from Dunfermline was sent out and took three days to restore the track. It was a very tricky operation with the men having to crawl under the wheels of the engines as they hung from the breakdown train. Snow was also a problem on the day of another, more serious accident, at Castlecary.

*Lumphinnans Junction – lines going to Cowdenbeath Old, Cowdenbeath New and Kelty*

That day, December 10th, 1937, is one which Dave Mackie will never forget .'I remember I was on back shift, two till ten, and I was on the messenger job that week.. This day was a terrible storm of snow and wind and we were sitting in the foreman's office having a cup of tea, when the phone rang. The foreman answered it and was writing the message down when we realised something was wrong. He told us there had been a smash at Castlecary with the Dundee to Glasgow, which was worked by Thornton men: Donald Macaulay was driving, Mr Fleming was fireman and J. Ingles was the guard. The phone rang again and we got some news as to what had happened. The four o'clock from Edinburgh Waverley had run into the back of the passenger train and telescoped three carriages .We got word that the driver of the Thornton engine was safe and the fireman was in the signal box, but there was no news of the guard. However, he was up front of the train, assisting passengers. The driver of the train, with a big Pacific engine 37, was D. Anderson, and he and his fireman were safe, but there were some passengers killed. The Thornton driver had spinal injuries. With the impact, he was thrown out of the cab window onto the grass banking. Fireman Fleming just got to the signal box to carry out Rule 55 immediately on being stopped, when the Edinburgh train flew past and hit the standing train.

*Coal train contrasting with snowy background*

Colonel Mount, who was in charge of the inquiry, had very high praise for Fleming on his alertness. Had he been two minutes quicker, he would have averted this disaster, but the blizzard and the deep snow would make that bit from the engine to signal box much more difficult than in normal conditions. The Edinburgh driver was taken into custody and was first charged with manslaughter, but was released later. I think it became clear that it was very severe weather conditions, and human element failure that caused this terrible disaster. After the case was wound up , Fireman Fleming was highly recommended for his part in the way he had carried out his duties and was later promoted to Loco Inspector. Later I landed in digs with a Master Coach Painter and Sign Writer, who had been given the task at Castlecary to sign-write the names of the dead on the coffins in gold paint'.

One of the people killed in the accident was Hugh Sharp whose father owned the Hill of Tarvit mansion ,now owned by The National Trust. Hugh, a director of several companies in Dundee, had served in the first world war, been awarded the Military Cross, .The Croix de Guerre and the Italian Military Medal. Because it was such a snowy day, he made the fateful decision to travel to Cardross by train to meet his fiancee. His library, one of the finest in the district, has been bequeathed to The National Library of Scotland.

# KIRKCALDY HARBOUR BRANCH

The harbour at Kirkcaldy had a rail connection as early as 1846 and survived till 1984. About 1910 when the harbour was enlarged and modernised a swing bridge carrying a railway track was built over the dock gates. When they were closed, the pug which belonged to Kirkcaldy Town Council would work the wagons over the bridge to the quays on the other side. There were sidings serving Hutchisons Maltings and Flour mills, Mackintosh's cabinet works, a stone dressing yard and an electric power station.

*Kirkcaldy Branch Line . Note the gradient*

Originally the branch, which had a gradient of one in twenty one, was designed to be worked by horses but after several accidents, a stationary engine was installed 'for safety and economy' and the wagons hauled up and down by ropes. In one incident, a wagon load of coal had collided with empty trucks, smashing several of them and throwing the coal over the pier wall. The Fifeshire Journal reported in March 1849 that the driver, with trucks with coal bound for the whaling ships, lost control and jumped off 'leaving them to chance'. In October the following year, the paper told of a driver who turned the screw brake the wrong way and a runaway truck hit a horse and cart breaking the horses legs and smashing the cart. The driver, the report said, 'escaped and absconded.' Sometime after 1870, the method of hauling by engine and rope ended and steam locomotives came into service, but they weren't immune from disaster.
In the early 1900s an engine ended up in the harbour and so too, on November 12th, 1954 , did engine 68341 driven by James 'Inky' Adamson. He escaped unhurt.

*The rescue team arrives. It took three engines to carry the crane needed to lift the engine*

*The J88 being unceremoniously rescued*

# BURNTISLAND RAIL DISASTER

Perhaps the most dramatic accident in Fife happened in 1914. At 4.50 am on April 14th. that year, a goods train running late was shunting on to a siding in Burntisland to let the London Aberdeen express through. The whole train except for the engine had cleared the main line when the express, its engine an Atlantic type weighing one hundred and ten tons smashed into it, left the rails and plunged over on to the embankment twenty feet below the permanent way. The driver and fireman were killed but of the twelve people injured, only four were hurt seriously enough to require hospital treatment.

The signals at Burntisland Junction cabin were set for the express to go through but those at Burntisland East were against it. The goods driver didn't see the express till it was only two hundred yards away. A fireman was at the signal box at the time and spotted the train before the signal man did but it was too late to do anything. It was not full daylight and the driver of the express would not have been able to tell which road the goods was on because of the curve in the track. It was this sharp curve which contributed to the accident. The glancing blow to the goods train was enough to upset its equilibrium and, according to an eye witness, 'the engine rose up in the air like a bird, and cutting through a parapet wall, shot over on to the links in a shower of sparks and escaping steam.'

*The amazing thing about this picture is that the railings are intact and undamaged.*

People living near the line were wakened by what they thought was the noise of an earthquake and the reflection of flames against the walls of their houses. The guard, who was able to escape from his van as it lay on its side, managed to put out the fire with an extinguisher and with the help of buckets of water from onlookers. Some passengers escaped through windows, others through spaces made when the carriages split open. One man was thrown into the air and then trapped by wreckage and had to cut his boot off to free himself, one was thrown out of the window by the force of the impact, another who had been sleeping stretched out on a seat Some passengers having breakfast in the dining car were saved from injury by the tables which prevented

*It's hard to believe that people crawled unhurt from this carnage.*

*Operation clear up.*

*Back on the rails again*

them being thrown out of their seats. Others, incredible as it seems, slept through the entire incident and were concerned only about how soon they could continue their journey. The rear, unharmed carriages of the train were detached and most people were able to do so by seven o'clock that morning.

Breakdown trains from St Margaret's and Cowlairs were early on the scene and both lines were blocked, traffic being diverted by Inverkeithing, Dunfermline and Thornton. The Commandant of the Station Ambulance Corps was one of the first on the scene and he crawled under the wreckage among the escaping steam to find out if either the engine driver or fireman was still alive. A large squad of men spent all day trying to recover the bodies of the men who came from Aberdeen. Both were married and the fireman had five children aged between eleven years and six months. Their coffins were taken in a special coach, first to Thornton, then to Dundee and from there by Express to Aberdeen.

The Fife Free Press reported a 'continuous stream of traffic from all over the district.' Thousands of people, on foot, on bicycles, by motor car and horse driven carriages of every description thronged the roads from Kirkcaldy and Kinghorn. The wreckage was covered with tarpaulin but an even bigger crowd was expected on the Sunday when the task of lifting the engine was to be carried out and extra police were to be drafted in. The reporter comments wryly that 'it is a strange commentary on human nature that within a stone's throw from the scene of death and wreck, the shows which annually congregate on the links for the spring holiday began to arrive on Thursday and ...Monday will see the Links turned into a show ground with all the fun of the fair.'

*Some of the men involved in the recovery operation*

## SPORTS AND PASTIMES

The statistical account, hand written in 1947 gives a picture of village activities, many of which still survive today. There was a curling club, founded in 1865, its club house and pond being on the banks of the Ore at the south end of the village. Much later, electric lighting was fitted and a cement surface was laid on the pond, with the power to flood it to the required depth. This was not very successful and the development of ice rinks in Kirkcaldy and Edinburgh made curling no longer dependent on either season or weather. The club was 'thoroughly representative of the village and District and has taken part in all the annual events of impor-tance. Their annual supper and initiation Ceremony is an event in the social life of Thornton.'

The bowling green, situated at the back of Station Road School was laid in 1930 and the first president was elected the following year. Money to buy the land for the green and club house was raised by private subscrip-tion 'and other means' and play has continued every year since then without a break. There was no class dis-tinction and the first committee included P,R. Donald, the famous school master, the doctor, insurance agent, joiner, hotel owner and coal merchant . Some of the club's collection of silver, the Dow, Dougall and Wilson Trophies, date from when the club started. The original club house, too, remains but extensions have been added over the years. A women's group was inaugurated in 1958 and the club membership of well over a hundred is evenly divided between men and women It is very much a family affair with husbands and wives and in some cases three generations of the one family taking part There is a junior section which has sadly dwindled to three, but they are very keen and their youngest player on record is nine years old. Jim Hepburn, the Club Secretary recalled how when he was at school, children were chased away if they even dared to look in at the gate. Now they are encouraging more youngsters to join and looking forward to their seventy fifth anniversary in 2005.

*The 25th Jubilee Opening 1955. Mrs Wilson throwing the jack, watched by husband D. Wilson,*
*first president in 1931 and president in 1955*

The Orr and Lochty Angling Association was formed in 1897 and some years later a hatchery was started on a pond at East Finglassie farm steading and the Lochty Water was stocked from time to time. In 1795, the Statistical Account reported the existence of plenty of different kinds of fish, salmon, pike and burn trout. A report from 1883 said that anglers came by rail 'and otherwise' to fish the Ore which, unlike the Leven, was unpolluted and trout were abundant and in good condition. By 1947, the chronicler complained that the number of trout caught in both Orr and Lochty was much less than in days of unpolluted water, before industrial refuse was deposited in these streams. John Dow remembered his uncle Jock landing the last trout caught in the Lochty in the early sixties and how ' the Lochty was running red' with pollution from the Westfield open cast plant. The Orr's pollution came from the coal mines. After that, competitions were held on Loch Leven and John recalls going fishing, at the age of eight, with his grandfather. They landed on the island in Loch Leven and took home a baby jackdaw. They made a pet of it but eventually lost it to their cat.

Thornton's Homing Society had eighteen members in 1947, an increase from the eleven who began in 1927 .

Some of those had previously been members of Milton and Rosslyn clubs. Birds competed in England and France with varying success and, during both wars, played 'a valuable and valiant part.' Jock Traill, an engine driver who retired from the railway when he was sixty, and whose interest in pigeons began when he was at school, describes the sport as it is now.

'My interest began when I was at School. I used to go to my Gran's in Broxburn for my holidays and my uncle kept pigeons. I started in 1951 and have about twenty five pairs plus about thirty young ones. I've had a lot of success in competitions and have dozens of trophies, being the first in Scotland for two years running. One bird flew from Nantes in France a distance of about six hundred and twenty miles and the other nearly seven hundred miles from Niort. It was released in France at six on Saturday morning and was back in the loft at ten twenty on Sunday morning. The birds are taken to Kennoway for ringing and marking, then go by road and ferry to France, leaving here on the Tuesday and arriving there on Friday. The birds' speed depends on conditions, a north

*Jock Traill with some of his trophies*

wind keeps them back. Because of that success I've been all over Scotland judging and been involved in social events. It's brought me a lot of happiness.

Last year I nearly gave up, though, my loft was broken into by young vandals and fifty two birds were killed, even the young ones in the nests. They know who did it but there wasn't enough evidence to charge them. A whole years breeding work was lost and I didn't have any birds to sell. I got a lot of letters of sympathy and gradually I've built up again. It's not so strong a sport as it used to be, it was mostly in mining communities and as the pits closed and miners moved out the sport went gradually down. There weren't so many railwaymen involved.

The Homing Society disbanded a few years ago through lack of members, though there are still about eight fanciers in the village who have joined other clubs in Kirkcaldy, Glenrothes and Coaltown of Balgonie. After I retired I worked as a lollipop man for three years but then I gave up and concentrated on my birds. There's racing every week in the summer. The old pigeons race from April 23rd to July 5th. The young ones are just trying to find their wings in May but by August they'll be ready to start racing. We take them to Sighthill in Edinburgh to begin with. We lose some to birds of prey. We've got Helen Eadie, one of our local members of the Scottish Parliament , supporting us and the Parliament are debating the need for a cull because of increasing numbers of hawks and other birds of prey. Sometimes nests have been found with as many as fifty rings in them, all that's left of our young birds. They put the numbers in the papers so people can know what happened. Not long ago, Billy Kay interviewed me and Stuart Young, another pigeon man, and the talk was broadcast on Radio Scotland. He would like to do a programme on dog racing but most of the old men who were involved with that are gone.'

Our 1947 correspondent would not have approved of such a programme. He found a serious cause for complaint in greyhound racing. 'The filthy state of our street and pavements' he wrote, 'are the results of the hounds being travelled up and down the village, to the disgust and defilement of the populace.' The track, complete with electric hare, was set up in 1930 and omnibuses and motor cars brought people from far and near. A Totalisator was installed by the local authority which appointed both the auditor and the electrician to make sure the government got its share of the betting revenue. The track was started by a Mr Brown, who had a billiard room in Thistle Street in Kirkcaldy, and Mr McLaren whose two brothers were engine drivers at Burntisland .

*War Memorial gates*

The money to buy Thornton Public Park, covering twenty two acres and originally part of the Balbirnie estate, was raised by subscription and the Highland Games Committee contributed five hundred pounds towards the cost of eight hundred and thirty five pounds. A public meeting, summoned by handbills, and attended by about one hundred and fifty people was held on May 9th, 1919, to consider a memorial to those who died in the Great War. The land was bought from Captain Charles Barrington Balfour CB, and a committee elected . In June 1920, this committee which included John Allen and PR Donald, resolved to provide an ornamental gateway with bronze tablets inscribed with the names of the war dead. Captain Balfour had agreed to perform the opening ceremony but unfortunately died before the opening day and his place was taken by Sir Ralph Anstruther of Balcaskie, the chairman of the North British Railway. The names of the dead of the first war were inscribed on one side and later those of the second were added on the other. The ceremony took place on September 24th 1921, PR Donald read the Roll of Honour and a lament was played by members of the Coaltown of Balgonie brass band. Representatives of local organisations including ex-servicemen were present.

The park was also the venue for football matches and for the annual Thornton Games. In 1947, the Football Club had been going for fifty years with its own team and with new young players coming up. The Hibs started as a juvenile and junior team and was very successful till the outbreak of war in 1939. It had to be suspended, but raised enough money to build a club house which was situated in the public park near the football pitch . It was opened by J .S. Martin, Secretary of the Fife Junior Football Association, who was a railway clerk at Sinclairtown station. There was also a railway football team, Thornton Loco, at one time.

*Thornton Loco: Fife Amateur Competition, Winners and finalists 1953 – 57*
*D. Yardley, J.McCrae, K. Youngson, J. Johnstone, Dick Graham, J. Currie, R. Addie*
*J. Richards, J. Mitchell, Willie Currie, Stewart Davidson, Alan Hardie*

*Thornton  Railwaymen's Golf Club 1935.  Back row –J. McBayne, T.Grieve, W. Wilkie, W. Provan, J. Scott,*
*Middle row – R. Reekie, T. Spinks, J. Robertson, G. Reay, J.T. Greig, R. Scott, W. Simpson, J. Patrick.*
*Front row –A. McLean, J. Jamieson, J.R. Fletcher, P. Aitken, J. Cunningham, D. Jamieson,R. Cunningham, W. Bell*

with Jim Williamson in goal and backs Jock Scott and Andrew Stark. Centre half Tom Graham became station master at Kelty and finished at Aberdeen. During the second war, half of the park area was taken over for food cultivation

Another sporting club that lost some of its land to food growing was the Golf Club. The first course was laid down in 1921 on land belonging to the farm of Mid Strathore but it was only rented on short lets and three or four holes were subject to regular flooding. The membership rose to one hundred and fifty and in 1935 a permanent home was found. Land , originally rough grazing close to Thornton Station, was bought from Colonel Balfour of Balgonie. In early days most members were miners and railwaymen who after a twelve hour working day would cut grass, keep the fairways playable and even on occasion, chase cows off the green. During the war, three holes were confiscated for ground to grow cabbages and an anti-tank trench was constructed on part of the ground 'to the detriment of the players' as our unknown writer puts it. After the war new greens and bunkers were needed and new grass laid and this work was carried out by club members. The membership dropped to fifty after the war but rose again to three hundred in 1970 when the course was enlarged to thirteen holes and plans were going ahead for a full eighteen hole course. This was achieved in 1975, at a cost of £26,000, with a course covering one hundred and fifty acres, full time green keeping staff and facilities for another two hundred members. There was also a flourishing ladies club.

As well as membership of golf and bowling clubs, there were ladies only organisations - The Women's Rural Institute, The Railway Women's Guild, The Church Guild and the Order of The Eastern Star. In the year 2000, the WRI is still going strong having celebrated its seventy fifth anniversary. Isabel Grant joined when she came to Thornton with her engine driver husband fifty years ago. The Rural had so many members it was held in the Crown ballroom at that time. Most railway men were gardeners and The Railway Staff Association held a horticultural show, usually the first Saturday in September each year in the Palace of Arts, Bellahouston Park in Glasgow. Isabel was not a member of the Staff Association but won countless prizes for her craft work. Grace Duncan was a Committee member for a number of years.

'I had to go through on a Friday night to set up the show. We had to get a bus to Kirkcaldy, two trains to Glasgow, and a car met me at the other end. It was difficult trying to get on buses carrying great stalks of rhubarb and stuff for the show. We stayed in a hotel overnight and were there before nine o'clock on the Saturday morning before the competitors started coming in. There was a bus laid on to take people from the station to the exhibition. Railwaymen came from all over Scotland, from Carstairs, Perth, Dundee, Inverness and from all the depots in Glasgow. The place was crowded with prize winning vegetables, chrysanthemums, dahlias, begonias, fruit, wine and flower arrangements. A lot of Thornton men competed successfully and the women entered the sewing and baking classes. Mrs Balfour, who lived to be one hundred and seven, and whose husband was an engine driver, was a regular winner for craft work at local and national level. The prizes were pathetic, just a shilling or two, but you didn't do it for the money. Davie never grew stuff for show, never took special care of his vegetables, but he still won prizes. You could take your stuff home again or else it was sold for the Association's funds.

We had a Railway Club in Thornton. My father and two other men got together and got a loan to buy the building and the members built on a big hall at the back. It was always mobbed at the weekend, with Bingo for the older ones and disco for the youngsters. A lot of men joined it so they could be involved in bowls, golf, angling and the Horticultural Society competitions but the membership went down gradually and expenses went up. The rates alone rose to eight thousand pounds a year so it had to close.'

The club was a great loss to the village. When Isabel Grant came to Thornton first they lived in Ritchie's Building and Andrew used to go to the club across the garden in his slippers. 'Everyone met there,' she said,' we all had our sprees there and wedding and silver wedding parties.'

*Thornton Railway Women's Guild Banner*

*The Fife Coast Express at Crail station. It ran regularly to Glasgow and Edinburgh. Sir George Sharp's father was a driver and he and his fireman used to sleep in one of the carriages at Anstruther. George had to go down at eight o'clock in the morning on the Edinburgh train with his father's piece.*

*Thornton Station on the last weekend of the Leven to Thornton service*

One of the advantages of working on the railway was the possibility of free travel and reduced fares. On Sundays in summer whole families would go to Lundin Links on the Fife Coast Express, taking a picnic and building fires on the beach to make tea. On the very last train trip from Largo to Thornton the Grants brought home a waiting room seat and a picture of Culzean Castle.

Grace Duncan recalled going for holidays to Spey Lodge in Aviemore. It had been an overnight stop for drivers but was made into a lodge for holiday makers. It was very basic, with rooms no bigger than a railway compartment, iron beds and an iron safe in every room but it was an ideal jumping off place. Later on , of course, people's horizons widened and travel throughout Europe became common. After her husband died, Isabel Grant travelled across Australia by train, a mammoth undertaking and not quite what she expected. No-one had warned her that there were no sleeping berths and people had to provide their own blankets to cope with the freezing night time temperatures. She boarded the train in a summer outfit and with only an overnight bag and sat and shivered till another lady recognised her plight and invited Isabel to cuddle under her blanket.

The most important event in Thornton's social calendar, the Highland Gathering, was held on the third Friday in July. Before holidays abroad became the norm, people from Glasgow flocked to Leven during the two weeks of the Glasgow Fair. There was only one way to get there - by rail - and extra platforms had to be provided to cope with the multitude. By 1900 the Gathering attracted an audience of 50,000 and more and William Crawford, the secretary of today's Games Committee can recall crowds of ten to fifteen thousand. In 1853 the games had been open only to residents of Markinch, Dysart and Kinglassie and consisted of foot, sack and 'bell' racing; hop step and leap; throwing the hammer and putting stone and quoit playing. One description of a game said that ' a goodly number of well dressed chiels, armed with quoits of unusual diameter were upon the play ground where a spirited and well conducted game was decided after about two hours hard labour.' On the same day, the proceeds of the Greasy Pole were 'equally divided among a portion of imbeciles from a southern village who had the spirit to shake the pole in place of climbing it, as should have been done, for the prize.' In 1855 there was dancing in the school afterwards at the cost of two pence but no stalls, booths or vehicles were allowed into the playground. Prize money was over £200 at the beginning of the

HE TRAINS ON "BOVRIL"

PROF. BERT POWSEY.
THE WORLD-FAMOUS HIGH DIVER.

century- high stakes for the men who competed . The Earl of Rothes was the Chieftain in 1913 when the attractions included Cumberland wrestling, pony trotting, tug of war and caber tossing as well as the usual races and dancing competitions.

There were side shows and menageries. William Crawford remembered some of the more spectacular acts. Professor Powsey had his clothes set alight and did a high dive act into a tank of water, diving down with flames trailing at his back. Blondini performed his high wire act, wheeling a barrow holding a young girl across the wire. One year, Blondini's wife who was his partner in the act, was unwell and Sheila McKay took her place. Sheila was a dancer with the circus and was at home on holiday in Coaltown of Balgonie. Today, although in her eighties, she still teaches dancing and is in demand for lectures and interviews because of her vast knowledge of many dances which are fast disappearing. Sideshows for the Games today are provided by Codona. The games still take place with competitors coming from all over Scotland but with only a fraction of the numbers and in recent years the event has been plagued with bad weather. In 2003 the Thornton Highland Gathering, which is a member of both the Fife and the Scottish Games associations, will celebrate its one hundred and fiftieth birthday.

# THORNTON PARISH CHURCH

The church has played an important part in the life of the community since it was established in 1835. At that time, the village had about five hundred inhabitants and permission had already been given by the Kirkcaldy presbytery for them to build a chapel. A committee was set up and a subscription list opened. The ground was given by the laird, James Balfour of Whittingham, who also donated twenty pounds. The stone came from Balbeggie by kind permission of the Earl of Rosslyn and the chapel opened on December 27th, 1835. People had to pay rent for their pews at that time and this, along with church door collections, helped to pay the minister's salary. Before he got his money, however, the precentor, beadle and cleaner had to be paid and payment made for any necessary repairs which had been carried out.

In 1847, Charles Balfour of Balgonie gave ground for a manse and it was erected the following year at a cost of two hundred and ten pounds. The money was borrowed from Mr Balfour and the minister agreed to pay the 3% interest in lieu of rent. During its first forty years the church had eight incumbents but in 1876, Reverend Duncan MacFarlane Wilson began a forty eight years long ministry. We know that in the eighteen thirties the village water supply came from well houses, and the minister was apparently no better served. In 1884, he is asking for a toilet for the manse and though there is no record of its being supplied, it was 1889 before a bath was installed.

By 1896, the population had grown so much that the church, which seated three hundred, had become too small and two wings were added to cope with a congregation of five hundred. A range of money-making activities helped to raise the money necessary – bazaars, concerts and lotteries with prizes which included, at various times, jewellery, bicycles, a sewing machine and even a donkey. The Balfour family continued to give monetary support and in 1900 four communion cups were bought with the help of one of their donations. In 1910 a new organ was purchased and electric light installed. By 1923, the congregation had increased to seven hundred and seventy four and the present church hall was opened in 1931.

In 1897, members of the Free Church in Thornton decided to have their own meeting place. They built a hall in Station Road in 1897 and appointed Thomas Orr as their first minister. In 1906, their church was completed, and named the Thornton United Free Church. Three years later, all Parish and United Free Churches joined to become the Church of Scotland and the building was renamed the Orr Memorial Church . At the same time The Parish Church became known as Thornton Old Parish Church. In 1954, the two churches were united with James Rankin, the minister of Orr Memorial Church, being inducted to the joint charge. He was followed in 1971 by Reverend Robert Hugh Drummond and in 1981 by Reverend David Gatt. Over the years, the chancel was completely refurnished with the help of various church organisations who donated gifts and money. In 1962, the Memorial Church building was converted into a Children's Church and with the accent on youth work it became a centre for family recreation. At that time, Thornton's population was approximately three thousand and of those one thousand two hundred were members of the church. Eighty per cent of the school population was actively involved in the church's Youth Education Programme. Unfortunately the Children's Church is now unused and almost derelict.

On 25th June, 1972, two stained glass windows in memory of Harry K. Brown and gifted by his wife, were dedicated. Designed and installed by a young Kelso artist, the windows depict, in a modern style, the Creation and the Resurrection and also includes a pit head, representing one of the chief industries of Thornton. In 1981, the Women's Guild celebrated its fiftieth anniversary and the following year the church railings and gate were replaced. The work was carried out by boys at the engineering class at HM Institution, Castle Huntly, Longforgan as part of their community projects, thanks to William Gordon, former Deputy Inspector of Prisons in Scotland and session clerk of Thornton Church. Another window of delicately coloured stained glass for the vestibule was gifted in 1985 by Mr and Mrs Henderson of Kirkcaldy. Mrs Henderson had for many years taken charge of the village Brownies. In that year, the church celebrated its one hundred and fiftieth anniversary.

In a booklet produced to mark this event, May Philp, a teacher and an outstanding daughter of the village, whose father was an engine driver closes by saying, 'Maybe our building has no claim to beauty but its quiet dignity with its lovely trees graces the village street. The first committee members began it all with much foresight and were fully conscious of their beliefs. Long may this spirit remain with us.'

# SCHOOL

No trace remains of the earliest school in Thornton, but in 1841 a school was built by public subscription on the Main Street. A second school in Strathore Road and originally owned by Dysart School Board is today home to the public library. A third school opened in Station Road in 1904, at a cost of £5,640.00 and with accommodation for five hundred and forty one pupils . The extent of population growth can be seen by the need for the Strathore Road school to be used for a time as an overflow from the Station Road school. The 1841 school building was converted and its date plaque incorporated into what is now the village hall. At one time it was used for picture shows and it is believed that the cine-projector is still in the building, hidden behind one of the partitions. In the thirties, there were nearly five hundred children in Thornton School and the village had an amazing array of shops and businesses – grocer, butcher, baker, hairdresser, chemist, jeweller, tailor, painter and decorator, joiner, cobbler, chimney sweep and even a golf club repairer. And of course there was the Co-operative Society and no less than two hospitals.

Old school records make fascinating reading. One hundred and fifty years ago, candidates for the post of teacher had to undergo an examination by four Church of Scotland ministers. The School House, as it was known then, was available for let for teaching music and dancing or any other purpose within its charter but lessees must not 'allow immorality within the gates.' The minister's sensibilities were taken into account by the removal of the 'school necessary' to the north side of the property so it would be out of sight of the manse. Careful managers even sold the school 'dung' to the highest bidder. Repairs to the school buildings were paid for by subscription and the managers displayed their independence when they refused to agree to a demand by Mr Balfour of Balgonie that he become a permanent member of the committee. This was in spite of his threat to withdraw his annual subscription of five pounds. In 1856, a concert to raise money for school funds sold seven hundred and thirty eight tickets and three years later, the sum of one hundred and forty pounds was considered sufficient to build a school master's house of three rooms and a kitchen. In 1862, however, the committee still had not decided to go ahead with the building. In 1869, the records show that Mr. Gibb was a candidate for the teacher's post. 'After studying him in his Redding School, the deputation decided that he had both brains and knowledge without which we fear a teacher cannot do much good.'

Thornton's most famous headmaster was P.R. Donald who came to the school in 1892 and remained there till he retired in 1928. Donald's interests included Freemasonry, curling, philosophy and poetry and his grandson has recently published *A Rustic Symposium,*a book of the dominie's poems. Donald was secretary of the Thornton Curling Club and of the Fife branch of the Educational Institute of Scotland and acted as Registrar for the Thornton area. He was very witty and two excerpts from the school log book demonstrate his unusual approach.

*December 23rd. 1893.* This week the scholars have tried their hand at decoration. In view of Christmas they have expended some labour in decking the school and even the school railings with evergreens , but quantity rather than arrangement plays a somewhat too prominent part in their ideas of the beautiful. As they, however, seem thoroughly satisfied with their efforts, criticism while it might improve the quality of subsequent attempts would certainly mar the pleasure of the present one.

*15th June, 1894.* Grammar in Standards V and VI is being neglected. Except for the fact that scholars have to be examined in this subject I would never teach it, as the mass of meaningless words under the name of parsing, ought to be relegated to the limbo of inane absurdities that, to some extent at least, have departed from the sphere of educative effort.

Donald was also famous for his copperplate handwriting, a skill which he taught his pupils and at least one of those had cause to thank him. Mrs Jessie Christie Wood Farmer, whose relatives R. Wood & Sons, had a joinery business in Thornton, taught at the school for a time before marrying a marine engineer from Leslie and emigrating to America in 1923. As a member of the organisation The Daughters of Scotia , she began work with the Nationality Rooms at Pittsburg University. These eighteen rooms, representing nationalities from early American to Yugoslavian, were provided as 'settings for the kind of education the faculty wanted to provide'. Mrs Farmer's skill at calligraphy led to her setting out citations, inscribing awards and formal invitations and to fashioning frontispieces for books presented to distinguished visitors. Her career culminated in her appointment as Keeper of the Archives of the Nationality Rooms.

## THE JOHN MENZIES CONNECTION

*The following document demonstrates , to use a railway metaphor, the fascinating sidelines which appear from time to time and divert you from the main track.*

TELEPHONE
CALEDONIAN 2491 (8 LINES)

TELEGRAMS
HANOVER · EDINBURGH

# JOHN MENZIES & CO. LTD.

HANOVER BUILDINGS · ROSE STREET,
EDINBURGH · 2.

Mrs. A. McMillan,
THORNTON JUNCTION BOOKSTALL.

21st October, 1958.

Dear Mrs. McMillan,

This historical book - "The House of Menzies" - has been compiled to mark our 125th year in business and our centenary as bookstall lessees.

The Directors feel that its contents will be of interest to our staff generally, since the loyal service of our employees throughout the years has contributed largely to the eminent position of John Menzies & Co., Ltd., today.

I therefore have great pleasure in asking you to accept this copy of the book, with my compliments.

Yours very truly,

*John M. Men...*

Chairman.

Mrs McMillan, nee Nan Dryburgh, and Euphemia (Fym) Collins worked in the Menzies bookstall for many years, serving the travelling public with papers and magazines. Sir George Sharp recalls how, as a boy, he was employed to carry a tray with books and papers and paraded past waiting trains.

'Malcolm Campbell's fruit and sweet stall was on the south side of the Leven passenger dock. Greta Page was the employee and they also had a boy with a tray moving along the trains. Sadly for me, Duncan Campbell's (son of 'Jeck' Campbell) sales of chocolate – Cadbury's Bournville etc was much greater than the return on my paper and magazine parade. On one occasion, a passenger gave a wee porter named Simpson a small three penny bit to buy a penny paper. Thinking he was in line for a good pauchle (tip), he hurried back with the paper and the two pence change. The old lady took the paper and the money and handed him a pan drop. The scene in the porter's bothy was hilarious. Dave McKay, his great friend and subsequently a shunter at Townhill and then manager of a hotel in Cowdenbeath and the Kingswood Hotel in Burntisland, had tears running down his cheeks. No wonder we treasure the memories of yesteryear when service, discipline and punctuality were the underlying guidelines of our commitment.'

For nearly a century and a half, John Menzies book stalls have been an integral part of railway stations. Menzies opened his first book shop in Edinburgh in 1833 and founded a business which made his name one of the best known in the country. From book selling and publishing he branched into newspaper distribution. In 1857 he set about acquiring bookstalls on the Scottish railway lines. The stalls at the two chief railway stations in Edinburgh were in the hands of non- Edinburgh firms and John foresaw that if a Scottish bookseller did not attempt to secure the Scottish bookstalls they would pass into alien hands. If all Scottish bookstalls were to be controlled by outsiders, the Scottish book trade, he knew, would be seriously affected.

On February 28 , 1857, he wrote to the directors of the Scottish Central Railway, offering to take "the stances at Perth, Stirling, and Bridge of Allan" for three years, at respective rents of £25, £25 and £10. Other companies were approached with similar offers. Within a few weeks of the contracts being signed, the first John Menzies bookstalls greeted the railway traveller.

By the end of 1857 he had bookstall contracts for the lease of all bookstalls on the Scottish Central line; he had placed offers for the bookstalls at the North British Railway Edinburgh terminus, and the stall at the North British and Edinburgh and Glasgow Railways' Edinburgh terminus; he had the rights for the stall at the Scottish North-Eastern Railway Station at Aberdeen; had applied for sole bookstall rights for all Scottish North-Eastern Railway Stations, including branches, from Aberdeen to Perth; had requested sole rights for all stalls on the Edinburgh, Perth, and Dundee Railway between Perth and Ladybank; and had made a firm offer to the Dundee and Arbroath Railway for stall rights on the Dundee and Arbroath line and the Dundee and Perth railway. Within another year he had the leases of bookstalls on every line from Edinburgh to Aberdeen

In  The *House of Menzies*, a history of the firm  published in 1958, tribute is paid to bookstall staff whose work demanded 'stamina, resourcefulness, a lot of plain common sense and, most of all, a sense of humour.' Menzies was an early promoter of female  workers. The Bridge of Allan stall was suggested as a trial for 'some respectable young woman who might employ herself with her needle' between dealing with customers. Sadly, like so many of the stations it served,  the John Menzies empire has gone.

*Steam coach Highland Chieftain*
*Driver J. Paterson, Sen, Porter Bob Gillespie, Fireman D. Thomson*

# STRIKE

*' The early history of the railways is full of stories of death and injuries to drivers and firemen caused by the carelessness, incompetence and greed of railway owners, who fought any attempt to introduce safety measures that cost money, who refused to reduce working hours to tolerable limits and who always paid the absolute minimum wage.'*

**Brian Murphy -   ASLEF 1880 – 1980, A Hundred Years of the Locoman's Trade Union**

Many railwaymen were  involved in varying degrees in political activities. Different grades had their own Trades Unions, with the National Union of Railwaymen accepting all grades. Most drivers and firemen, however, were members of The Association of Locomotive Engineers and Firemen, their union founded in 1880 when it became apparent that the existing unions did not suit the precise requirements of the loco  men with their own specialised skills, and exposure to their own particular dangers. The Union's first test came in 1887 when  an express ran into the back of a stationary train. The driver and fireman were accused of manslaughter despite the fact that they had a clear road and that the block signalling system was out of order. Up till that time powerful railway companies  with expensive lawyers had always loaded the blame on to the engine men, and men were imprisoned for  accidents caused by faulty equipment. By 1887, however, ASLEF had sufficient funds to pay for a top lawyer and the men were acquitted.

*Front row l-r : J. Moodie, T. Spinks, A. Hunter, W. Gillespie, A. Scott, T. Graham, A. Sharp, P. Aitken,*
*L. Wilson, D. Balfour, J. McKenzie, D.Laing*
*Second row  includes: J. Scott, , A. Thomson, R. Forbes, T. Storrar, J. Wright, J. Hughes, A. Hughes,*
*D. Briggs,G. Reay, A. Graham, W. Scott, W. Mackie*
*Third row:  R. Barnes, W. Murray, A. McKenzie, J. Foote, P. Robertson*
*Back row includes J. Moyes, M. McIntosh.*
*Other names unknown*

The rail companies continued to provide huge dividends for their shareholders but made no attempt to improve safety and conditions of work and rates of pay deteriorated. In 1911 the threat of a national rail strike saw Churchill sending troops to deal with strikers and two railwaymen in Llanelli were shot dead. Needless to say this strengthened the strikers resolve and helped to end working class support for Liberal government. In 1919, during a strike by the National Union of Railwaymen over the principles of an eight hour day , ASLEF came out in sympathy and left the country without railways for ten days.

In 1923, the railway companies demanded a new wage agreement which would have lowered the wages of footplate men. They maintained that wages were too high compared to other industries and in spite of the fact that profits were higher than they had ever been, demanded that wages should be reduced. Poverty in other areas was to be matched with financial hardship for railway employees. The strike lasted nine days, and in November 1924, John Bromley, General Secretary of ASLEF, was elected as Labour Member of Parliament for Barrow. The 1926 Strike has been too well documented to need repeating.

During the second war, loco men were exempt from the armed forces. Their work was too imortant and skilled drivers could not be replaced. In 1941, the LNER instituted a Railway medal for acts of railway gallantry and among the recipients were W. Stewart from Methil and J. Lackie of Ladybank.

The nationalisation of the railways in 1948 brought hopes of an industry where men would have some control over their wages and working conditions, but as in other areas the government made the mistake of not bringing the workers into partnership and were not prepared to take advantage of the expertise and practical insight of the men who knew how the job ought to be done. Unions also had to fight for an occupational pensions scheme which was common in public service but was not seen to apply to newly nationalised industries.

There were a number of unofficial strikes in the early fifties but the longest strike in the Union's history, lasting seventeen days, was in 1955 and was about wage differentials. Since 1948 and nationalisation, the footplate men had seen the differences in their wages compared to other grades whittled away and though the sums of money awarded were not large the strike settlement re-established the principle that skill and experience must be rewarded.

In January 1955, the plan for re-organisation of the railways had announced that there would be no new passenger or suburban steam locomotives and the building of all new steam locomotives would cease within a few years. In fact, the last steam engine ever to be built for British Railways was the Evening Star, named in 1960. The following year, Dr Richard Beeching was appointed Chairman of the new British Railways Board at the incredible salary of £24,000 per annum. In the year 2000, the country is still suffering from the ruthless effects of his scalpel. Union membership was reduced by two thirds by 1980, which is an indication of the reduction in the industry as a whole. New technology and computerised systems have made today's engine driver an operator rather than a skilled craftsman but the comradeship built up over years of struggle has vanished with steam and remains only in societies like the Thornton Railwaymen's Group.

*June 1955 ASLEF STRIKE*
*Back row : James Ewan, T.Temple*
*Front row : Alex Abercrombie, Hugh Docherty,*
*James Davidson*

# THE NATIONAL UNION OF RAILWAYMEN

Railway unions, in common with other trades, grew out of the need to regulate hours and wages. Working weeks of one hundred hours or more were commonplace and because many jobs had a set wage, regardless of hours spent, up to a third of train staff time could be unpaid. Railway companies were driven by the need for profit and as long as footplate men could be held responsible for accidents, they saw no need for regulation. The twenty four hours in a driver's day belonged to the rail companies and according to one' they are all ours if we want you to work them....'. If a driver fell asleep at his work, that was his problem and complaints of exhaustion were met with instant dismissal. Most rail workers lived in company houses so dismissal meant the loss of the family's home as well as its livelihood.

The first strikers in 1836 were imprisoned for a month for breach of contract and put to the treadmill for six hours a day. Until 1871, a number of strikes took place and usually ended, as they did in all industries, with men either being sacked or forced to return to work under harsher conditions. In that year, railwaymen joined with shipwrights and engineers to support the demand for a nine hour day and this culminated in the formation of first large scale union, The Amalgamated Society of Railway Servants. The Scottish branch of the society was formed the following year. In Scotland, men worked even longer hours and for less pay than in England but because they worked in smaller groups, early attempts at unionism didn't have the same power. The opening of the Forth and Tay rail bridges meant a vast increase in traffic and consequent overwork for staff. By the time of the first strike in 1891, there were over thirty five thousand railway workers in Scotland, and the most important result of the their industrial action was the acceptance of a maximum nine hour day.

In 1913 , the existing rail unions amalgamated into the National Union of Railwaymen and it included all grades: clerical staff, hotel domestics, waiters, storemen, printers of tickets and timetables, even those who made crutches and wooden legs for disabled railway workers.

At depots or yards with a large concentration of workers there could be several branches of the NUR. Thornton had three branches - Number One, the largest, catered for all grades; Number Two and Three membership was made up of signalmen and supervisory and salaried staff. Willie Munro was for twenty years Secretary of the Methil Branch which included the docks and Cameron Bridge to Largo; Methil, Leven and Wemyss Castle. The Thornton branch had five hundred members, Methil two hundred. In additions there were branches at Dunfermline, Kirkcaldy, Inverkeithing and Ladybank.

Among those who were secretaries of Thornton branches of the union were J.Shepherd, guard, R. Murray, boiler smith, W. Bett, driver and A. Williamson, guard.

John Todd, driver was Secretary at the same time as his brother Alex was Secretary of the Thornton branch of ASLEF. John subsequently became running foreman at Thornton Locomotive Depot and Alex filled the same post at Dunfermline. Sadly, with the run down of the railways, the NUR declined and it no longer exists in the Thornton Area.

*Centre Pilot. May 27, 1939*

*Driver George Galloway (the Dug) and Fireman James Paterson, one of the cleverest men at the depot*

# THORNTON TODAY

Thornton today is once more a sleepy little backwater of a village. Until 1983, in spite of the loss of mining and railway workings, its main street was one of the busiest in Fife. As the main thoroughfare between Glenrothes and Kirkcaldy, thousands of lorries, vans, cars and buses thundered through it every day. But in August that year a new bypass was opened and the decrease in traffic was accompanied by a corresponding decrease in trade for local shopkeepers.

In the seventies a consortium of business men, engineers and former miners was set up to investigate the possibility of re-opening the Rothes Colliery. Opened in 1958 by the Queen, the first and probably the only monarch to go down a pit in Britain, it began in a blaze of confidence about the future of Fife as the mining capital of Britain. It was designed to be the show piece pit, with an estimated work force of two thousand five hundred and a projected working life of one hundred and fifty years. It closed in 1962, without ever having got near its targets. Only one thousand men were employed and hardly any coal was produced. As well as geological and industrial problems, water poured in at the rate of thirty five thousand gallons per minute and both shafts and underground tunnels were flooded .

The consortium believed that the problems were surmountable and wanted the mine to be pumped out to enable surveys to be made. They forecast a working life of thirty years and the provision of seven hundred jobs, but both the Coal Board and The Scottish Office rebuffed all overtures and the scheme fizzled out. The fifteen hundred foot flooded shafts were used as testing grounds for submersible equipment for the armed forces but for thirty years the twin winding towers stood as a unique monument to failure. The towers were finally demolished and the rubble dumped down the shafts which were then capped. Many people were of the opinio- that the towers could never be destroyed because of their construction but engineers discovered that they were made from pre-stressed and not as had been thought post-stressed concrete. Demolition by explosives was considered the best option and in March 1993, the towers - two hundred foot high and containing twenty two thousand tons of concrete finally disappeared.

*The new hump yard with Rothes Pit Tower in the background*

In October 1984 a new diesel locomotive maintenance depot was opened by Councillor Robert Gough, Convenor of Fife Regional Council and Jim Cornell, Deputy manager of British Rail who drove a locomotive through the tape and into the shed. The new unit had the capability of emergency fuelling and maintenance of Diesel Multiple Units and held fifteen of these. Built on the site of the old wet ash pit, where steam engines used to have their fires cleaned, it was the first unit in Scotland in which the eight maintenance staff were trained in both mechanical and electrical work on diesel locos.

*The opening of the new station*

1991 brought the promise of a new station at Thornton, the first to be built in Fife since Rosyth Halt was opened in 1917. The recently launched Fife Circle passed through Thornton but passengers from there had to go to Kirkcaldy or Markinch to catch a train. The station was to be situated near the site of the old goods station, would have drop off points, taxi facilities and parking for forty cars. The money for its construction was to come from Fife Regional Council, Scotrail and Glenrothes Development Corporation with some grant assistance from the European Regional Development Fund. The investment by Fife Council was part of their policy to upgrade and maintain existing station facilities for the benefit of the travelling public.

Under the Transport Act 1962 (Amendment) Act 1981, known as the Speller Act, British Rail was allowed to open lines and stations on a trial basis and close them again with only six weeks notice if they failed to attract adequate passenger levels. Even before it opened, the station caused great controversy. Its first suggested name, *Glenrothes South*, roused a storm of protest from the Thornton community which was horrified that the historic name of Thornton should disappear from the railway map. The answer they were given was that basically Glenrothes were putting up about a third of the money and unless the station was seen to be serving the town, and benefiting the residents and businesses, the Corporation would not be allowed to contribute. Eventually *Glenrothes with Thornton* was chosen. Sir George Sharp fought a long and ultimately unsuccessful campaign, in private and through the local press for the name *Thornton for Glenrothes*. The principle had been accepted already when Markinch was renamed *Markinch for Glenrothes*. The station was in Thornton, a mile away from the boundary of Glenrothes and three miles from the town centre. Other protests came from disabled groups who complained of lack of consultation during the planning stage and the difficulties of for wheelchair users. It is understandable that Thornton, so long the railway capital of Fife, should feel slighted. The first passenger railway station opened there in 1877 and as late as 1956 sixty passenger trains per day ran between Kirkcaldy and Dundee, rising to eighty four in the summer months. It closed as part of the Beeching cuts. The new station opened on May 12, 1992, seventeen minutes late because of a points failure at Inverkeithing.

Before long there were stories of bewildered travellers looking for the town centre under the belief that they were actually in Glenrothes. A former resident of Thornton asking at Waverley Station for a ticket to Thornton was told that the station was at Glenrothes but that there was a good bus service. None of the parties concerned in planning and development can be proud of their ineptitude in this matter. Consumer protection for travellers appears to be a myth. Certainly there is car parking at the station and a taxi rank. Unfortunately, there are no taxis and though there is a fairly good bus service to Glenrothes there are no notices giving this information. The first steam engine through the new station since the introduction of diesel power was the Thornton based Union of South Africa during a Scottish Railways Preservation Society trip from Aberdour to Carlisle.

In 1996 opencast development took place on a one hundred and fifty acre site at Balbeggie with the promise of twenty jobs. Seventy per cent of its output was to go by rail from Thornton to Longannet, the other thirty to Methil. It didn't bring any jobs to the village because it was all machinery and the company's own men were employed, but it didn't bring any of the disturbance feared by the villagers. Aldra Stocks was a member of Thornton Community Council and was on the Liaison Committee for the opencast . She said there had been very little noise or traffic problems and only once was there reason to complain to the Council about dust. Sprinklers were installed and the problem disappeared. More worries surfaced when the pit bings at the Randolph were to be removed because people remembered the fumes from burning bings which turned polished brass green overnight but that worry, too, was unfounded.

There are still miles of sidings and coal heaps lying in the yard but they are no longer seen as part of Thornton. Four years later, the open cast mining has finished and plans are well ahead for the transformation of the area by landscaping, providing a pond and woodland walkways. Once that has been done the countryside to a great extent will have returned to an agricultural and rural landscape that would not have been unfamiliar to the eighteenth century Thorntons and Balgonies.

*Steam returns to Thornton. No.9 between Lochty and Largoward*

*The end of a dream for some, of a monument to failure for others.*
*The Rothes pit towers are demolished.*

*Steam retraining at Thornton.*
*Scotrail Chairman John Cameron ( front right)*
*with Tam Galloway, Harry Aitken,*
*Peter Hutton, John Grey and John Bruce,*
*traction inspector .*

*(reproduced by kind permission of The Courier)*

*John Cameron on the footplate of his engine,*
*The Union of South Africa , built in 1935 and*
*originally called The Osprey.*
*In 1937, coronation year, five engines were chosen*
*to haul the Coronation Express and were each*
*named after a Commonwealth country.*
*Engines sometimes were given different names*
*(such as Bon Accord - see page 97)*
*for special trips*
*Note the springbok logo.*

# RAILWAY POETS

## ROBERT RUSSELL

*Robert Russell, a railway clerk and the son of a guard, lived in Station Road ,Thornton near what is now number forty. He died in a casualty clearing station near Merville in France on December 12, 1917. A little book containing thirty six poems still survives but gives no indication of who put the collection together or when it was printed.*

# THE PIPES AT YPRES.

Not the hills o' the north or the steep highland glens
Hae seen sic magic that music hae made,
It gave courage that nane but a Scotsman kens,
When the pipes at Ypres played.

Fresh was the foe and the highlanders few,
Worn and weary; tired and dismayed,
The bandsmen, they thought of a tune that we knew,
And the pipes at Ypres played.

The tune that they played woke each laddie's soul,
That great courage and power betrayed
To our trenches so stealthily the enemy stole
But the pipes at Ypres played.

Nerved to the core each highlander stood,
The enemy's approach so calmly surveyed
They'd stop them and turn them if anyone could,
While the pipes at Ypres played.

In a mad, awful wave the enemy came,
That not e'en wire entanglements stayed,
But stopped at the kilties, to whom be the fame,
Yet the pipes at Ypres played.

*This little poem would have been one of the last Robert Russell wrote.*

## FOR CHRISTMAS 1917.

Dear-------- it is with honest pride,
This day I send this card to you;
From feelings that I cannot hide,
To wish the old wish here anew.

May thy life be full of pleasures,
Bound by friendships loving spell;
All that thy heart fondly treasures,
Be thine, and always with thee dwell.

I wish you health and happiness,
I wish you joy and friendship true
Long life and all its loveliness,
Is your dear boy's wish for you.

## STEVE ROBB

*I am indebted to Sir George Sharp for these poems. Steve Robb was a railway foreman at Kirkcaldy. He wrote this after Sir George lent him a copy of Robert Russell's poems. Steve also made models of Anstruther fishing vessels and some of these were displayed in Kirkcaldy Museum & Art Gallery*

When o'er this book ae blink ye tak
Ye only get a taste o it
And many times ye maun gae back
E'er ye possess the best o it.

Dear Sir, wi thanks baith big and mony
I send ye back this book sae bonny
And if it has been damaged ony
In my possession
Weel pleased I'll pay the fine, dear crony
For my transgression.

Tho lately pressed for leisure sair
(An books like this need muckle care)
I managed ilka day tae spare
An oor or twa
Tae fill ma noddle wi its lear
And man, it's braw.

## FIFE BUDDIES

We're canty bit folkies in Fife
An we stick the gither sae weel
That we somehow aye hang by our heids
While there's many hang by the heel.

We're fond o a drap and a sup
The makin an savin o gear
And Lord when we get it we keep it
An jist live on the sicht o't per year.

We like a bit cleish and a claver
An we're no sae averse tae a lee
An we tak guid care that the ither
Is never fund oot, d'ye see.

We're canty bit buddies in Fife
We're clannish as abody kens
We've met in a pairts o the earth
By twas and by threes, even tens.

We ta'en up oor place in the world
An maybe it's ill for the rest
That we stuck sae like thieves tae each ither
Well, we're only Fife buddies at best.

It may be bonnie there awa
Wi hill an loch an river
But true tae Fife we'll shout hurrah
Fife an its fowk forever.

## THE BONNIE LAND O FIFE

See, here's a happy little man
Who wants to brighten life
By spinning yarns and weaving rhymes
About the realm of Fife.

The Kingdom lads are pawky chiels
Douce, honest men, though sly
You know the jokes o city folks
Who spell Fife F L Y.

That quality is somewhat old
Since this world was begun
All people that on earth do dwell
Look after number one.

All Fifers know the ten commands
Indeed they keep them well
And certainly they don't forget
The eleventh - man mind thysel.

For happy homes and kindly hearts
Gae search where'er ye may
Few can compare wi those that dwell
Between the Forth an Tay.

I've stood on Italy's sunny peaks
Where splendid views are rife
Yet still prefer, frae Falkland's tap
the bonnie land o Fife.

## BETTY FORRESTER

### An Ode to Thornton Junction, Fife

All is gone - not a sign of life
And grass now covers the ground laid bare
It's sad to remember the bustling life
That seethed on platforms and buildings there.

And in my mind's eye the myriad rails
In all directions twist and stretch
And in the distance I see the steam
And hear the clanging from the engine sheds.
The passenger trains, express and slow
The specials, the troop trains, passing fast.
The freight and goods - and twice per day,
The lines all cleared as the "Fish" shrieks past.
The staff; all friends, remembered well,
The Porters, Shunters, Inspectors, Guards,
Signalmen, " Reliefs", Cleaners, Clerks,
Coping with shifts and working hard.

The other day I travelled through,
And in nostalgia for the place,
I watched approaching landmarks pass -
Then missed it - 'cos there's now no trace!

*Betty's poem was printed in  the Spring 1997 edition of Penfriend,*
*the railway pensioners newsletter.*

# APPENDIX 1
## THORNTON LOCOMOTIVE DEPARTMENT - ROSTERED JOBS CIRCA 1935
*Information supplied by Sir George Sharp*

## GOODS TRAINS

| | |
|---|---|
| 12.01 am | Thornton to Aberdeen |
| 12.20 | Portobello |
| 12.45 | Kelty |
| 1.00 | Conditional |
| 1.05 | Carlisle |
| 2.05 | Conditional |
| 3.00 | Conditional |
| 4.05 | Perth |
| 4.10 | Leslie |
| 5.15 | Leslie |
| 5.15 | Anstruther |
| 5.30 | Cupar |
| 6.10 | Glencraig |
| 6.10 | Methil |
| 6.20 | Frances |
| 6.45 | Kelty |
| 7.05 | Townhill |
| 8.20 | Kirkcaldy |
| 8.45 | Lochty |
| 9.00 | Burntisland |
| 9.00 | Conditional |
| 10.00 | Conditional |
| 11.00 | Conditional |
| 12.10 pm | Conditional |
| 12.50 | Dundee |
| 12.50 | Methil |
| 1.00 | Conditional |
| 1.50 | Francis |
| 2.00 | Glencraig |
| 3.00 | Conditional |
| 3.20 | Perth |
| 4.25 | Aberdeen |
| 5.00 | Conditional |
| 5.30 | Cupar |
| 6.10 | Kelty |
| 7.25 | Aberdeen |
| 8.00 | Conditional |
| 8.30 | Portobello |
| 9.00 | Conditional |
| 9.40 | Buckingham Junction |
| 10.00 | Glencraig |
| 10.00 | Conditional |
| 10.50 | Townhill |
| 11.05 | Conditional |

## ROSTERED PASSENGER TRAINS

| | |
|---|---|
| 6.31 am | Thornton to Inverkeithing |
| 6.45 | Leven & Edinburgh |
| 6.50 | Dunfermline |
| 7.40 | Edinburgh |
| 8.01 | Glasgow |
| 8.38 | Dundee |
| 10.02 | Dundee |
| 10.38 | Dundee |
| 11.57 | Edinburgh |
| 12.10 pm | Crail |
| 1.46 | Dundee |
| 1.50 | Dunfermline |
| 2.56 | Glasgow |
| 3.45 | Edinburgh |
| 5.24 | Edinburgh |
| 6.48 | Glasgow |

Steam coach, Methil Branch, two shifts 7am – 8pm

### STAFF:

**In 1935 there were 166 drivers,** 165 firemen and 40 cleaners, 3 shed foremen, 1 shed master, clerks, roster clerks, telephone attendants, fitters and assistants, boilermakers, plumbers, labourers, fire droppers, steam raisers, joiners, stationary machinery attendant, storemen and storekeeper, blacksmith, coppersmith, boiler washers and gland packers.

**The shed and coaling plant** worked three shifts as did six out of seven yard pilots; the carriage pilot did two and the sub pilot one.

**There were nine signal boxes:** Thornton Station had six men, West had three plus two book markers, Central, North, South, Randolph, Redford and Weighs each had three while East had two.

**In the yard** were inspectors, foremen, shunters, wagon examiners, greasers, pointsmen, signal fitters, lamp men and surface men.

**The station staff** included the station master, inspectors, porters, ticket collectors, telegraph operators and clerks.

**Thornton had five sub depots:**

| | |
|---|---|
| Anstruther - | 3 sets of men, 1 goods and 2 passengers |
| Burntisland - | 11 sets plus 4 pilots |
| Methil - | 11 sets plus 4 pilots and the Leven End pilot |
| Ladybank - | 7 sets plus 2 pilots and ballast pilot |
| Kirkcaldy - | 3 sets plus 1 pilot |

*SHED FOREMEN AND RE-DESIGNATED SHED MASTER:*
Old Shed : J. Ellis,    Wm. Liddle   New Shed:   J.R. Fletcher, J. Edmondson, J. Sneddon, T.F. McKay

## APPENDIX 2
## LONDON AND NORTH EASTERN RAILWAY COMPANY
Statement showing when the various sections of the Northern Division of the Scottish Southern area were opened. Many of the lines are sadly now closed.
*Information supplied by Andrew Henderson, former locomotive driver*

| MAIN LINE SECTIONS | DATE |
|---|---|
| Burntisland to Markinch | 1846 |
| Thornton to Crossgates | 1846 |
| Markinch to Cupar | 1847 |
| Cupar to Tayport | 1848 |
| Crossgates to Townhill Doubled | 1849 |
| Townhill to Dunfermline Upper, Single | 1849 |
| Charleston Branch Line opened for working by locomotive power | 1853 |
| Milnathort to Ladybank, Single | 1857 |
| Kinross to Milnathort Single | 1858 |
| Lumphinnans South Junction to Loch Leven, Single | 1861 |
| Charlestown extended from Merryhill cutting to the shore | 1862 |
| Bervie Line | Nov 1865 |
| Leuchars to Wormit and First Tay Bridge to Dundee and Camperdown | May 1878 |
| Tayport to Wormit | May 1878 |
| First Tay Bridge Fell | Dec 28th 1879 |
| Bervie Line Transferred to N.B. Rly Coy | Oct 1881 |
| Montrose to Arbroath Railway Goods Traffic | March 1st 1881 |
| Townhill to Dunfermline, Doubled | 1881 |
| Montrose to Arbroath Passenger Traffic | May 1st 1883 |
| Second Tay Bridge | June 20th 1887 |
| Forth Bridge to Inverkeithing | March 1890 |
| The Portion Between Inverkeithing and Dunfermline Lower Doubled | March 1890 |
| Inverkeithing Central to Burntisland | June 1890 |
| Cowdenbeath South Junction to Kelty South Junction | June 1890 |
| Portion between Kelty South and Kinross Junction Doubled | 1890 |
| Kinross to Mawcarse now part of Edinburgh & Perth Main Line, Doubled | 1890 |
| Kinnedar Branch, Oakley | July 1892 |
| Charlestown extended from Goods Station to Passenger Station and opened for traffic | 1894 |
| Glencraig Craighead and Dundonald Branches | April 1896 |
| St. Vigeans to Inverkeilor Doubled | June 20th 1897 |
| Lumphinnans East and Lumphinnans North New Loop | April 1901 |
| St. Fort to Glenburnie | Jan 1909 |

| BRANCH LINES | DATE |
|---|---|
| Thornton Junction to Leven  Single | 1845 |
| Kirkcaldy Harbour Branch | 1846 |
| Pettycur Branch | 1846 |
| Ladybank to Perth | 1848 |
| Dunfermline Upper to Alloa | 1850 |
| Alloa to Stirling | 1851 |
| Railway Goods Traffic | March 1st 1881 |
| Alloa to Tillicoultry | |
| St Andrews Old Leuchars | 1854 |
| Whitemyre to Kingseat Colliery | |
| Steelend to Gask Branch | 1858 |
| Kelty to Blairadam as a wagon road | 1859 |
| Balmule Branch tine made by Earl of Elgin and taken over Branch line by the West of Fife Coy along with Charlestown Branch | 1860 |
| Markinch to Auchmuty | 1861 |
| Markinch to Leslie | 1861 |
| Balmule Branch transferred To NB Rly Coy | 1862 |
| Rumbling Bridge to Kinross | May 1863 |
| Alva Branch | June 1863 |
| Kilconquhar to Anstruther | Sept 1863 |
| Tillicoultry to Dollar | May 1869 |
| Kelty to Lochore Mine | 1870 |
| Dollar to Rumbling Bridge | May 1871 |
| Kelty extended to Blairenbathie by NB Rly Company | 1875 |
| Townhill Branch between Townhill Junction and Lilliehill Junction | 1879 |
| Capledrae Siding to Westfield | 1882 |
| Thornton to Buckhaven | 1882 |
| Anstruther to Boarhills Sept | 1883 |
| Longcarse Branch | 1885 |
| Boarhills to St Andrews | June 1887 |
| Buckhaven to Methil | 1887 |
| Mawcarse to Bridge of Earn | 1890 |
| Kincardine Junction to Kincardine Station | Dec 1893 |
| Inverteil  Junction to Foulford Junction | March 1896 |
| East Fife Central Railway | 1898 |
| New Loop Lumphinnans Central and Cowdenbeath North with altered junction and Loop to Kelty | Jan 1900 |
| Steelend Branch extended | 1905 |
| Kincardine Station to Elbowend Junction | July 1906 |
| Lochore to Redford extension | 1909 |
| Thornton Junction, doubled | June 1910 |

## APPENDIX THREE
## NICKNAMES

Railwaymen are renowned for their wicked sense of humour and at least half of the drivers and firemen, as well as guards, yard staff, examiners and inspectors had nicknames. Some of these were even passed down from father to son. Dave Mackie was Young Swank to distinguish him from his father, Swank who was also known as The Ashpan King, while the Allans were The Ranter and The Young Ranter. Some names are easy to understand, like Hurricane Tam Thomson, who did everything at a rush, Buffer Lock Bill Oliver, Robert (Frosty Bob) Forrester and Diesel Jim McKenna.

Some were obviously derived from physical characteristics, like :

Baldy - W. Munro
Girn - A. Gourlay
Lantern Jaws - Millar
Two Ton - John Cummings
Darkie - W. Young
and Kipper Lugs - J.Finnie.

Others are a bit more obscure in derivation. Sir George Sharp was known as Fido. Other animals were:

The Hare - J. Lawson
The Cock - J. Moodie
The Fox – J. Traill
Tiger - J. Lawson
Buck - J. Taylor
Blue Flea - J .Duncan
The Bull - J. Dowie
The Hawk - D. Crystal
The Pelican - R. McDonald
The Clipshear - ? Cunningham
The Trout - T.Henderson
The Cod - W. Millar

Others , in a very mixed bag ,were:

Sailor - A. Brunton
The Duke - J .McDougal
The Count - A. Goodall
The Major - R. Moyes
The Admiral- H .Graham
The Packman - A.Cowan
The Dairymaid - Dempster
The Chemist - W. Milne
The Spiv - ? McFarlane
Squeaker - J. Thomson
Memory Man - R. Graham

The Undertaker - T. Graham
The Drummer - J. Moyes
The Docker - A. Mitchell
The Hangman -W. Robertson
Dixie - W. Barclay
The Hag - D. Page
The Sneck - H. Watson
The Snosh - T.Muir
The Skelf - A. Morrison
Spitfire - Math Brown
The Gint - G. McKaig
Becket - A. Dryburgh
The Tank - J. Sharp
Jinks - J. Jamieson
Monkey Wrench - W. Elder
Brose Knot or Granny -W. Lowe
The Livin Yin - W. Simpson
The Deid Yin - W. Simpson (no relation)
The Boreland Ghost - E. Walker
Pout - D. Henderson
Seek'nin' - R. Masterton
Foggy - G. Meldrum
Toffee Bob - R. McGregor
Baffie - A. Balfour
The Chief - W. Biggs
Tuck - R. Rougvie
Bimmy - J. Walker
Peazle - A. Wishart
Casey - J. Jones
Inky - J. Adamson
Hitler - A. McKenzie
Pie Wull- W. Allan
Boxer - J. Bain
Polly Ann - J. Wyness
Cocky Lee - J. Lee
The Inkspot - R. Black
The Barrel - W. Osler
The Conk - A. Cochrane
The Wimp - A. Williamson
The Pet Lamb - W. Dryburgh
Ah'm No Carin - T. Nairn
The Swistler - J. Bain

*For every one of these names there are stories, some apocryphal, a few unrepeatable, but it would take another book to record them.*

# BIBLIOGRAPHY

Markinch and Its Environs ............................................................... A. S. Cunningham. Leven. 1907

The Melvilles and The Leslies ................................................... William Fraser . Edinburgh. 1890

The Railways of Fife ..................................... William Scott Bruce. Melvin Press. Perth. 1980

The North British Railway ........................... David Thomas. David and Charles. 1969

The Road Between the Forth and Tay ......................... George Bennett. Markinch Printing Co. c1984

British Railways Past and Present ................Sanders & Hodgkins. Past & Present Publications 1994

North British Railway– New Tourist Guide........................... John Miller. Glasgow 1890

Thornton Parish Church 1835 –1985 ................................... M.G. Philp. Thornton Parish Church

Auchterderran of Yester-Year, volume 3 ..................... WEA Corrie Centre History Group

An Investigation into the Life of David Hatton ................... Jean Mackay. Kirkcaldy District Libraries

The Railway Gazette, March 1955

North British Railway Study Group Journals - various dates

Fife Free Press - various dates

The Dunfermline Press - various dates

British Rail Files – The National Archives of Scotland, Edinburgh

The Register of Sasines – The National Archives of Scotland, Edinburgh

The First Statistical Account 1794

The New Statistical Account 1845

The Third Statistical Account 1952

# PICTURE ACKNOWLEDGEMENTS

Grateful thanks for allowing us to reproduce the following photographs are due to:

The Peter Westwater Collection – pages 6,8,10,11,12,13, 15,16,17, 18,21, 22, 26, 27,29,33, 35, 36,37,39, 40,44,46,50,51 (lower) 54, 59,60,73,75,76,77, 78 78, 80,86.

Marshall Dickson: page 9,14 (lower), 28,53,55,74, 109.

Alex J. Donald: page 34,52

Mrs A. Hughes: page 7, 69

Mrs Grace Duncan: page 45, 85

Mrs Walker: page 54 (upper)

Alexander Campbell: page 57, 60 (lower), 76 top left.

Grant Baillie: page 98

Jim Hepburn, Thornton Bowling Club: page 81

Kirkcaldy Central Library: page 3 (lower) 68, 87, back cover picture

Dunfermline Press: page 63

The Courier: page 99 (upper)

Dr. John Cameron CBE: foreword; page 97, 99

Other pictures are the property of members of the Thornton Railwaymen's Group

The following maps are reproduced by kind permission of the Trustees of National Library of Scotland.

J. Blaue. Fifae pars occidentalis. 1654

J. Ainslie. The counties of Fife and Kinross. 1775

J. Thomson. Fife and Kinross. 1824

OS. Scale 1:10,560. Fife and Kinross. Sheet 32. 1854

OS Scale 1:2500. Fife. Sheet XXVIII.9. 1914

*No 9 near Aberdour, heading south, December 1993. Driver Alex Abercrombie, Fireman Pete Hutton*

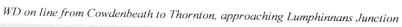

*WD on line from Cowdenbeath to Thornton, approaching Lumphinnans Junction*